Creative
Scrapbooking
With Your Computer

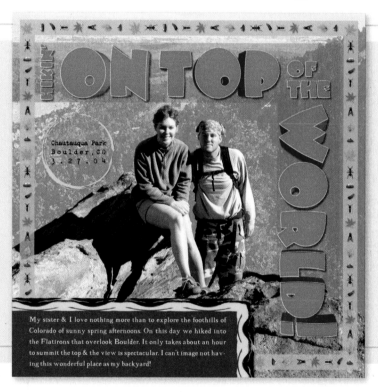

Chautauqua Park
Boulder, CO
3.27.04

My sister & I love nothing more than to explore the foothills of
Colorado of sunny spring afternoons. On this day we hiked into
the Flatirons that overlook Boulder. It only takes about an hour
to summit the top & the view is spectacular. I can't image not having this wonderful place as my backyard!

Simple tips and techniques for stunning layouts

**MEMORY
MAKERS
BOOKS**

Managing Editor MaryJo Regier

Art Director Nick Nyffeler

Designers Jordan Kinney, Robin Rozum

Art Acquisitions Editor Janetta Abucejo Wieneke

Craft Editor Jodi Amidei

Photographer Ken Trujillo

Contributing Photographer Jennifer Reeves

Contributing Writers Helen Bradley, Tonya Doughty, Veronica Ponce, MaryJo Regier, Michelle Shefveland

Editorial Support Karen Cain, Amy Glander, Emily Curry Hitchingham, Dena Twinem

Memory Makers® Creative Scrapbooking With Your Computer

Published by Memory Makers Books, an imprint of F+W Publications, Inc.
12365 Huron Street, Suite 500, Denver, CO 80234
Phone 1-800-254-9124

First edition. Printed in China.

09 08 07 06 05   5 4 3 2 1

Library of Congress Cataloging-in-Publication Data

Creative scrapbooking with your computer : simple tips and techniques for stunning layouts.
    p. cm.
    Includes bibliographical references and index.
    ISBN 1-892127-53-9
    1. Photographs--Conservation and restoration--Data processing. 2. Photography--Digital
techniques. 3. Photograph albums--Data processing. 4. Scrapbooks--Data processing. 5.
Digital preservation. I. Memory Makers Books.

TR465.C758 2005
745.593--dc22

                                                                    2005043877

Distributed to trade and art markets by
F+W Publications, Inc.
4700 East Galbraith Road, Cincinnati, OH 45236
Phone (800) 289-0963
ISBN 1-892127-53-9

Distributed in Canada by Fraser Direct
100 Armstrong Avenue
Georgetown, ON, Canada L7G 5S4
Tel: (905) 877-4411

Distributed in the U.K. and Europe by David & Charles
Brunel House, Newton Abbot, Devon, TQ12 4PU, England
Tel: (+44) 1626 323200, Fax: (+44) 1626 323319
E-mail: mail@davidandcharles.co.uk

Distributed in Australia by Capricorn Link
P.O. Box 704, S. Windsor NSW, 2756 Australia
Tel: (02) 4577-3555

Memory Makers Books is the home of *Memory Makers*, the scrapbook magazine dedicated to educating
and inspiring scrapbookers. To subscribe, or for more information, call 1-800-366-6465.
Visit us on the Internet at www.memorymakersmagazine.com.

This book belongs to

_____

This book is dedicated to scrapbook artists everywhere who dare to venture into the digital domain and beyond. A special thank you goes out to the featured artists herein who so graciously allowed us to showcase their computer-generated art with the hope of inspiring others to view their hardware, software and scrapbook creations in a whole new light. Many thanks to the product manufacturers whose products grace the pages of this book.

Introduction

Today's digital products have impacted and infiltrated our lives and are continually changing the way we scrapbook. In the past few years, I've met two schools of computer scrapbook artists: those who use their computer just to print photos, page titles and journaling blocks and those who've gone to 100 percent digital scrapbooking. This book was designed specifically for both types of scrapbookers.

Despite technology's daily advances, there will always be scrapbook artists—myself included—with an absolute physical need to cut and paste and create heartfelt pages by hand. And when you're not real fond of your own handwriting, the refined look of computer-printed page titles and journaling is a nice touch. Personally, I've used both Macs and PCs, scanners and printers in a creative capacity for well over a decade. But when I received a digital camera for my birthday two years ago, it stayed in the box. As a traditional-trained photographer with a trusty SLR I'd grown to love, the digital camera seemed not only frightening and intrusive but it seemed frivolous and ridiculous.

When I finally shot some digital images, I was so impressed with the photos and how easy it was to download them to my computer that I bought a new printer and photo paper so I could print the quality photos I had been accustomed to receiving from the photo lab. And I can't begin to tell you how exhilarating it was to create my first computer scrapbook page using page-design software. Oh what joy, what speed, what creative control! I am hooked on using technology to help me preserve memories, but the die-hard traditional scrapbooker in me will always find time to shoot film and cut and paste at my scrapbook workspace. Technology will not take away that physical need, but it has certainly enhanced the way that I scrapbook!

And that is what I want to share with you. This book is presented in a manner that both traditional and computer scrapbookers will appreciate. Similar to traditional scrapbooking, we go from paper to photos to lettering to page accents. You'll discover clever ways to create digital paper backgrounds and paper page accents. Then you'll explore the exciting ways to manipulate photos in a user-friendly manner, followed by all the fun you can dream of with fonts. And last, but not least, you'll learn how to create those wonderful page accents you've grown to love—all on the computer. Whether you are a traditional scrapbook artist or a digital scrapbook artist, I guarantee you will be inspired by fresh ways to use technology to enliven your scrapbook art. Enjoy!

MaryJo Regier
Managing Editor
Memory Makers Books

Lineco's PopArt Printable Album Pages can be inkjet printed for custom gifts and stylish computer-generated scrapbook page presentations.

Table of contents

Creating Perfect Digital Paper & Paper Accents, 20-43

Colored, shaped, postage stamp, torn paper, patterned paper, punched, vellum, word, textured, metallic, stitched, aged, embossed and painted paper backgrounds; slide mounts, library tabs, manila-folder pocket, paint chips and tag paper accents

Photo Manipulation Made Easy, 44-65

Simple, shape and silhouette cropping; tearing, mosaic, kaleidoscope, collage, tinting, distressing, saturating and de-saturating photos; artistic filters

Having Fun With Fonts, 66-83

Serif, san serif and script fonts; mixing, skewing, rotating, alternating, beveling, repeating, shaping, customizing, collaging and designing with fonts; font sampler

Crafting Digital Page Accents, 84-105

Baubles (beads, buttons, acrylics, jewels, rhinestones, watch covers); metallics (typewriter keys, metal-rimmed tags, stapes, anchors, eyelets, brads, paper clips, hatpin, letter charms, nailheads, buckles, hinges, barbed wire, bookplates, charms, decorative clips, bottle caps and chrome lettering); organics (wooden letters and accents, leather, rope, pressed flowers, shells, ferns); textiles (clothing label, printed ribbon, gingham, fibers, fabric, lace, rickrack and appliqués)

What is computer scrapbooking?

Computer or digital scrapbooking means different things to different people. On a basic level, it's using your computer to help create scrapbook page elements—such as page titles, journaling blocks and to print photos or clip art. On a higher but just as easy level, computer scrapbooking can encompass complete digital page design by layering backgrounds with photos, fonts and custom-made page accents with just the click of a mouse. How in-depth you use your computer for scrapbooking is a personal preference, but exploring your creative potential by pushing your hardware and software to their full potential certainly has its just rewards. Experiment, explore and have fun!

Traditional vs. computer scrapbooking

Both traditional and computer scrapbooking are satisfying and rewarding. By comparing and contrasting the two, you will see that the two types of scrapbooking are quite similar; what makes each different is you!

The key pieces of hardware commonly used for computer scrapbooking include a hard drive, monitor, keyboard and mouse. This sleek, budget- and user-friendly system is the HP Pavilion Home PC, with an a820n hard drive and an f1903 monitor. To round out the ultimate "digital darkroom" for computer scrapbooking, added peripherals include an HP Photosmart R707 digital camera and an HP Scanjet 4070 Photosmart scanner.

Traditional scrapbooking

- You participate in hands-on creativity at its finest
- Your page design is driven by your artistic vision
- Your results are highly personalized art
- Your results make great gifts
- You are getting good use out of your scrapbook tools
- You are using all of those scrapbook supplies you've purchased
- You can find fun new products almost daily
- You are preserving treasured memories that are easily shared and stored

Computer scrapbooking

- You participate in hands-on creativity at its finest
- Your page design is driven by your artistic vision
- Your results are highly personalized art
- Your results make great gifts
- You are getting good use out of your digital tools
- You are using all of those digital supplies you've purchased
- You can find fun new products almost daily
- You are preserving treasured memories that are easily shared and stored

Computer scrapbooking essentials

To experiment with and explore computer scrapbooking, you'll obviously need a computer hard drive, monitor, keyboard and mouse or a laptop computer. Necessary peripherals—any extra equipment you connect to your computer—include a digital camera and/or a scanner and a printer. It is likely that you will use the equipment that you have on hand for computer scrapbooking, but if you're in the market for new equipment, shop around for the best buy on equipment that will meet your needs as a scrapbooker. As in traditional scrapbooking, the quality of the products you use can help determine the quality and archival-longevity of the art you create.

The best computer system for computer scrapbooking will be one that is budget-friendly, compatible with your preferred software, have plenty of extra memory for large image files and a CD burner for archiving images and sharing your digital artwork. A monitor with at least a 17" screen is desirable to avoid eye fatigue and to accommodate the many windows you may have open at once while creating your digital art. A printer should be large enough to accommodate the size of photos or pages you want to print, have superior image quality and utilize fade-resistant and archival inks. You'll find more on printers on pages 10 and 11, and on page 12 we'll discuss software—the digital equivalent to your creative hands and mind.

Printers should be large enough to accommodate the size of photos and digital scrapbook art that you wish to print. HP offers a wide range of home-use printers perfect for your intended use. Featured left to right are the HP Photosmart 8450, the HP Photosmart 8750 and the HP Photosmart 2610 All-In-One (printer, fax, scanner, copier). These printers offer studio-quality color and superior black-and-white photo printing.

Digi-speak

If you're new to computer scrapbooking, it's a good idea to sharpen your knowledge of the language of image-editing software and the digital world, which have a language all their own. For your convenience, there is a chart of basic image-editing tool icons and tasks on page 108. On page 109, you'll find a glossary of terms used in computer scrapbooking to get you started.

Digital cameras

The foundation of all great computer-generated scrapbook pages is great photos. Many computer scrapbookers scan photos into the computer before creating digital art, but more often than not they are using digital cameras to save time. The benefits of using a digital camera include being able to view pictures immediately after taking them (and easily deleting less desirable ones) and easily transferring or downloading the images to the computer. Because these images are already in digital format, they're ready for editing, printing or publishing on the Web or copying to a CD. Spend some time experimenting with and getting to know your camera's functions and abilities for best results.

If you are in the market for a new digital camera, consider these key features when making a purchasing decision:

Resolution

Most digital cameras have a resolution between two and six megapixels. Higher resolution means more detail. A two-mexapixel camera is great for e-mailing images, publishing them on a Web site or making prints as large as 5 x 7". You'll need three mexapixels to print a clear 8 x 10" image and four mexapixels for a good 11 x 17" picture. Higher resolution also means you can crop a picture, print part of it at a larger size and still have a clear picture. However, if you raise an image's pixels higher than the camera's pixels that originally rendered or took the picture, your enlargements will look pixelated.

Optical zoom

More expensive cameras have optical zoom lenses that magnify the subject while preserving the same resolution. Less expensive cameras have digital zoom that magnifies the subject but at a lower resolution. Optical zoom lets you take a clear picture from a distance, and it's one of the most important camera features for most photographers.

Storage

A typical two-megapixel camera comes with an 8MB memory card that can store eight to 10 images taken at the highest resolution. You have to transfer the images from the full card to your computer before you can reuse the card. Even if your camera comes with a larger memory card, you'll still probably want to get a spare.

Size and weight

Smaller cameras are more convenient, especially for travel or shooting on-the-go, but may have fewer features.

Macro photo capability

A macro capability enables you to take extreme close-ups, useful for rephotographing old pictures.

Price

Digital cameras are more affordable than ever. Expect to pay about $100 for a two-megapixel camera without optical zoom. Cameras with 3x optical zoom cost about $300 for three-megapixel models and about $400 for four-megapixel models.

Batteries

Most digital cameras now come with rechargeable lithium batteries, which are more cost-effective than disposable batteries in the

Today's budget- and user-friendly digital cameras come in all shapes and sizes—from 35mm to compact to ultra slimlines—each with their own unique qualities and features. Shown left to right are Kodak's DX3500, HP's Photosmart R707, Nikon's D100, Konica Minolta's DiMage X50, Fujifilm's FinePix, HP's Photosmart 935, Concord's Eye-Q 5062 AF and Canon's Powershot A70.

Scanners

A scanner digitizes flat objects and photos and can come in very handy for inserting existing or heritage pictures into digital pages, adding document copies to computer pages and creating custom background "e-papers" and faux digital page accents. A scanner also makes it easier to share or e-mail images and artwork. If you already own a scanner, read the owner's manual to become familiar with the scanner's functions and abilities. Keep the glass surface clean and be careful not to scratch the surface when scanning three-dimensional objects.

If you're looking to buy a new scanner, you'll have three types of scanners to select from:

Flatbed scanners

Just like photocopiers, flatbed scanners have a flat surface suitable for pictures and paper. Most have adjustable covers so you can scan bulky items such as books and magazines. This is the most common scanner for at-home use.

Sheetfed scanners

More compact than flatbed scanners, sheetfed scanners feed pages through and pull them over a fixed scanning device. They are limited to single sheets of paper and photos.

Film Scanners

Some flatbed scanners come with transparency adapters, but dedicated film scanners are made especially for slides and 35mm negatives.

When selecting a scanner, consider these features:

Resolution

A scanner's resolution is measured in dots per inch (dpi). A scan made at a higher resolution creates a more detailed image. For good print quality, you'll want to scan at a resolution of at least 300 dpi. Naturally, high-resolution images take up more memory.

Bit depth

A scanner with a higher bit depth can recognize more color gradations and reproduce colors more faithfully. A 24- or 30-bit scanner is fine for everyday use, but a 36-bit scanner is better when you want the best reproduction of color photos.

Other features

You should also consider the scanner's speed, maximum document size (usually letter size for flatbed scanners) and connectivity (if your computer supports it, USB is better than a parallel connection). If available, look for color-correction scanners with scanning software that automatically restores the color of your faded photos, negatives and slides.

Price

Prices typically range from $50 to $200 for sheet-fed and flatbed scanners and from $180 to $300 for film scanners. Most scanners are PC- and Mac-compatible.

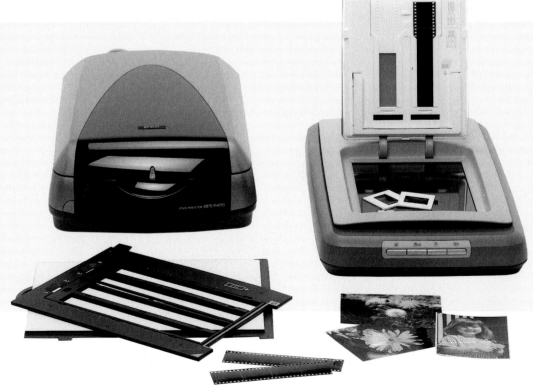

Two popular, high-quality and versatile home scanners include the Epson Perfection 4870 Photo scanner and the HP Scanjet 4070 Photosmart scanner. Both offer transparency units for scanning positive/negative film and transparencies.

Printers

The latest computer printers are faster, less expensive and produce better output than ever before. If you're using an old printer, it may be time for an upgrade. As a digital scrapbooker, you will want exceptional-quality printed images that will resist fading and yellowing and last for generations.

If you are looking to purchase a new printer, there are a number of things to consider to help you make an informed and happy purchase. First, determine what size paper is the largest you may want to print on. Then consider the archival quality of the printer's inks. You might also want to compare prices on the printer's consumable supplies, such as compatible ink cartridges and photo papers. Finally, ask to see sample prints, preferably on the kind of paper you intend or prefer to use.

Compact photo printers allow you to edit and print true-to-life photos at home or on the go. They're also ideal for printing computer-generated pages for small and mini albums. Shown left to right are the HP Photosmart 375, the Epson PictureMate Personal Photo Lab, the HP Photosmart 245 and the Canon CP-220.

There are three different printer types on the market:

General-purpose inkjet printers

If you want one printer to handle text for letters, color graphics for digital scrapbooks and photographs for sharing with relatives, an inexpensive inkjet printer may be your best choice. Many inkjet printers are practically giveaways, but ongoing expenses for ink cartridges and special paper add up quickly.

Multifunction printers

Most scrapbookers need a printer, but could also make good use of a scanner and a copier. Amazingly, you can now get all three functions in a single space-saving unit relatively inexpensively.

Photo printers

Whether you're printing old family pictures that you've scanned or the latest snapshots taken with your digital camera, you'll want prints that rival or exceed the quality of professionally processed photos. Photo inkjet printers fit the bill and some even print directly from a digital camera or memory card with no computer needed.

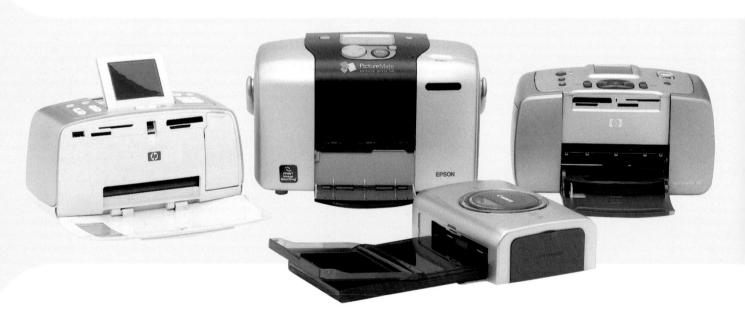

Ink and media compatibility

Most manufacturers of inkjet printers calibrate their ink, media and hardware to work together as a system, optimize hardware performance and produce prints of exceptional quality. Keep in mind that whichever printer you select, using the same manufacturer's ink systems and choice of printing media will ensure the best print results possible.

Typically, the more ink colors a printer prints with, the better. More colors translate to better subtle colors and tonal changes when your art is printed.

Today's dye-based and pigment printer inks are specially formulated for long-lasting results. Follow your printer manufacturer's recommendations for replacement inks as well as printing media for the best printing results possible and to prolong the life of your printer.

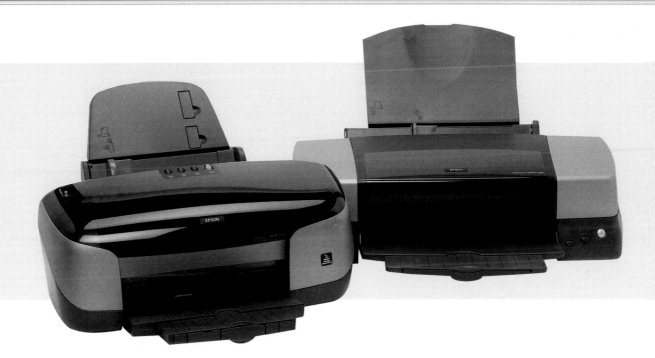

Epson's great array of printers offer exceptional print quality and excellent longevity. Featured left to right are the Epson Stylus Photo 960 and the Epson Stylus Photo 1280. Both printers are ideal economical choices; the 1280 is great for large-format printing up to 13 x 44", including 12 x 12" digital scrapbook pages.

Color calibration

Sometimes, the colors of photos and digital art that you see on your computer screen are not necessarily the colors you get when you print out your computer-generated photo art. The best way to solve the problem is to "calibrate" your monitor and not trying to change your printer's color settings.

To check for color-calibration accuracy, first print a photo with multiple colors in it, using a high-quality print setting and quality photo paper. Next, access your monitor's on-screen control buttons, usually found on the front of the monitor. If there's a color-temperature choice, set it to 6500K, which will make your monitor's desktop appear slightly more dim and yellow than usual. Follow this with adjusting colors as needed until the image on your screen resembles the printed image. Your digital art should more closely resemble what you see on-screen the next time you print.

Large format printers, like the Epson 2200 printer, can handle media as large as 13 x 44"—great for large scrapbook pages and family tree wall charts. Though this printer is geared more toward advanced amateur photographers and artists, it's a fine choice for home use if you want to make large photographic prints, and it's ideal for digital scrapbooking.

Software

You don't necessarily have to have image-editing software to create a computer-generated scrapbook page. Some digital scrapbookers create wonderful scrapbook pages in simple word-processing programs such as Microsoft Word. Others create stunning digital art using desktop publishing software. But if you want the maximum creative freedom to manipulate your photographs in a myriad of ways, the best choice for computer scrapbooking is an image-editing software program.

There are many fine image-editing software programs on the market. Sometimes you'll get free trial, mini and even full versions of some programs when you purchase a new scanner. If finances will allow, always opt for the full versions of the software. The learning curve will vary from person to person with any image-editing software program, depending upon your familiarity with the software and with photography, as well as your willingness to experiment.

Today's image-editing software programs are quite user-friendly and results-oriented. All include basic image-editing functions such as rotate, resize, crop, correct red-eye and convert color photos to black-and-white or sepia tone and more. Basic features also include the manipulation of different image formats, such as JPEG or TIFF as well as the ability to adjust the resolution of an image.

Daring and creative scrapbookers will cherish more advanced image-editing software features—from sharpness/blur control and creating collages to special-effect filters and photo edges. Users can even add elements like a lens flare, different backgrounds, lighting effects or artistic text to their photos.

There is a dizzying array of image-editing software programs available. Read the manufacturers' boxes to be certain the software is compatible with your computer system and that its key features are what you're looking for where computer scrapbooking is concerned. Most, if not all, software packages are geared for novices, professionals and everyone in between. Compare prices, user level and the learning curve involved, special effects and common features and technical support information for these powerful creativity tools, and once you've settled on a specific image-editing software package, spend an entire day learning its specific tools and the tools' functions and effects. Time spent at the outset will make for quick-and-easy computer scrapbooking!

More popular image-editing programs include Roxio's Photosuite Platinum 7, Broderbund's The Printshop Deluxe, ACD System's Acdsee7 Powerpack, and ArcSoft's Photo Impression and Photo Studio.

You'll also find many software products made specifically for the consumer scrapbooker to enhance your digital creativity. These include Broderbund's Click Art 400,000, Janlynn's Cre8's Photo-Suite Cre8, Nova Development's Art Explosion Scrapbook Factory Deluxe, Kaleidoscope Collections' Kaleidoscope Kreator, Ulead's My Scrapbook 2, HP's Scrapbook Assistant and ArcSoft's Collage Creator—as well as Provo Craft's PC Hugware CDs and The Vintage Workshop's Click-n-Craft theme CDs.

Widely used image-editing software programs include Jasc's Paint Shop Pro 9, Adobe's Photoshop Elements 3.0, Corel's Corel DRAW and Adobe's Photoshop CS (Creative Suite).

Printing mediums

Browse the shelves of an office-supply superstore and you'll be awestruck by the enormous range of photo papers available for printing your computer art—including gloss, semi-gloss and matte finishes. You can also print on cardstock, vellum and other assorted scrapbooking papers, but you will not get the superior image quality that photo papers will give you.

Photo-quality papers, whether with matte or glossy surface finishes, will give your digital art the look of professionally processed photographs. You can print pictures on letter-size paper and trim the individual images. If your printer supports them, you can print on 4 x 6", 5 x 7" or other precut sizes—including 12 x 12" and even larger when using roll paper and large-format printers.

Archival concerns and longevity

If you want prints that rival traditional photographs in terms of image quality and fade resistance, be sure to use the photo paper recommended for your printer model. Prints made on archival photo papers, stored in archival albums and protected from ultraviolet light will last a very long time. Most printer manufacturers make their own brand of papers that usually produce the best image quality and print longevity.

In addition to fade resistance, you should also consider how well the paper resists yellowing. For that, the paper should be acid- and lignin-free. If the paper's package doesn't say acid- and lignin-free, the paper is probably not archival.

Among the top-of-the-line photo papers and photo sticker sheets available are Ilford's Photo Printasia Premium Photo Glossy Paper, Kodak's Glossy Photo Paper, Epson's PremierArt Matte Scrapbook Photo Paper, Janlynn's Cre8's Computer Crafts for Scrapbooking paper, HP's Premium Photo Paper, Epson's Semigloss Scrapbook Photo Paper, Epson's Premium Glossy Photo Paper and Epson's Self-Adhesive Photo Stickers.

If you are using photo papers that are not marked "archival quality," protecting digital photos and digital art is easy with Krylon's Preserve It! The spray can help prevent moisture, fading, early aging, ink runs and damage from smudges.

How to make your first computer scrapbook page

Armed with a basic understanding of what computer-generated scrapbooking is—as well as some available hardware, software and paper and ink mediums to make the job easier—you're ready to make your first digital scrapbook page. For the purpose of this tutorial, we've used Adobe Photoshop CS. Most image-editing soft-ware programs have similar features, but if the tools mentioned don't seem familiar to your specific software, check your software manual or do an onscreen Help search in the software to identify the same or similar tools. With that in mind, let's begin!

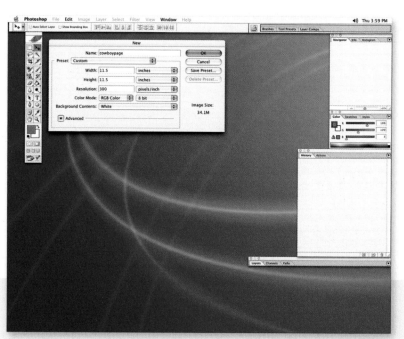

illustration A

Create the background

1 Launch or open your software to create a page background in the desired size. Choose File, New and select the width and height of your page. Set resolution at 300 pixels/inch. For standard printers, make an 8½ x 11" page. For large format printers, create an 11½ x 11½" background. Set color mode for RGB color (illustration A).

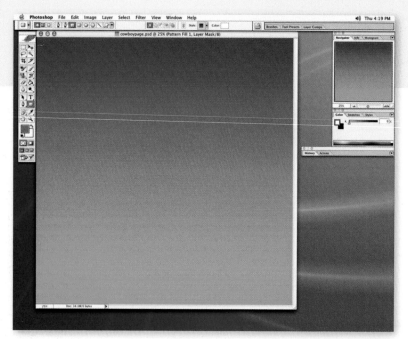

illustration B

Style the background

2 To create a solid background, choose a foreground color (in this case orange; illustration B), then use the Paint Bucket tool to color the background.

To create a patterned background, select Edit, Fill, and from the Use dropdown list, choose Pattern and select a built-in pattern (illustration C).

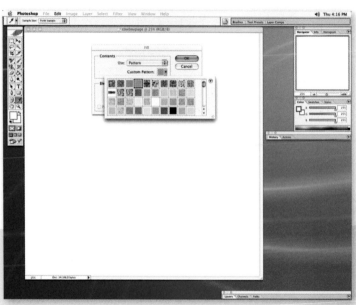

illustration C

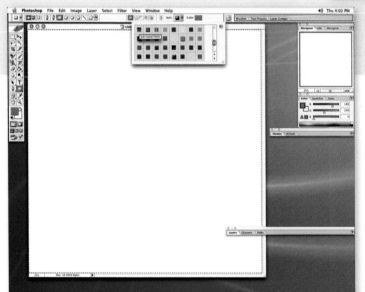

Or click on the Rectangular Marquee to select all, click on rectangular shape, then select a Style from the dropdown list (in this case Sun Faded Photo) and drag it to the background (illustration D).

illustration D

Add the images

3 If you wish to add color blocks or borders to the background first, click on the rectangular Shape tool and drag the pointer across the page with your mouse to draw your shapes. Select a foreground color and use the Paint Bucket tool to fill in the shapes with color (in this case black). For photos, click File, Open to open the images you want to use on the page. You can go ahead and crop or resize the images first or drag the Rectangular Marquee tool across the part of the images you want to use. Choose Edit, Copy and then Paste the images onto the background. Use the Move tool to position where desired. Finally, use the rectangular shape tool and click on Style to add drop shadows, beveled edges or mats to the photos (illustration E).

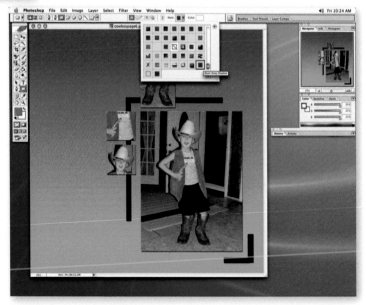

illustration E

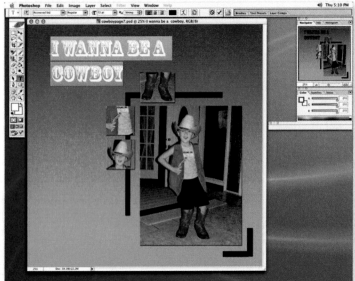

illustration F

Add title

4 Click on the Text tool. Select a font (in this case Rosewood Std), font size (in this case 72) and color (we used black) and then type the title directly on your background (illustration F). Elaborate or fancy fonts work best for page titles. To find a font that goes well with your page theme, highlight your title by drawing your mouse over it and experiment by changing to different fonts for the look you desire. Use the Move tool to position the title where you want it on the page.

Add journaling

5 Follow the same steps you used to create the title to add journaling. Select a simple font for the journaling text (we used Cochin at 15-point size; illustration G) to make the journaling easier to read and so it won't compete with the title. Based on your page design or the look you want to achieve, select left-, center- or right-justified text formatting for the journaling (we used left-justified). Use the Return key on the keyboard to experiment with bumping words down a line if needed for visual appeal.

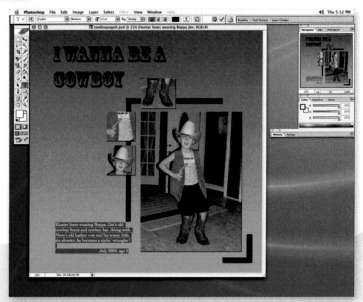

illustration G

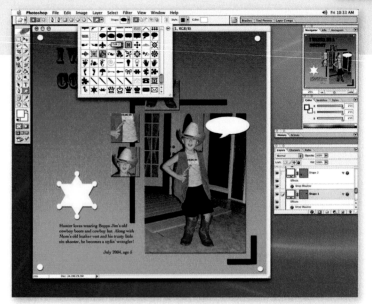

Add page accent shapes

6 Use the Shape Marquee tool to select shapes that work well with your page theme. If your software is new, you can use the Append command (the tiny arrow on the dropdown menu will reveal the rest of the shapes by theme) to load all the shapes that came with the software. Click on a shape (in this case, a conversation bubble and sheriff's badge were used; illustration H) and then use your mouse to draw the shape in the desired size directly on the page; use the Move tool to position where desired. Use the Ellipse shape to draw small circles for digital faux brads as seen on the corners of the page.

illustration H

Style page accents

7 Click on the Freeform Shape tool to select the shape you wish to style then select a Style from the dropdown menu (in this case woodgrain; illustration I) to add texture and dimension to the shapes.

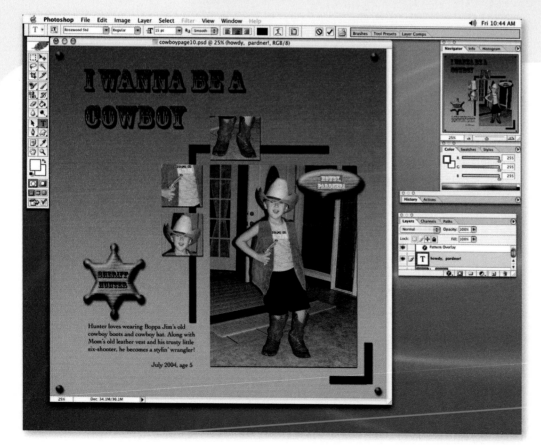

illustration I

Add text to page accents

8 Click on the Text tool and select a font, size and color. Then type directly over page accents to personalize them (illustration J) and use the Move tool to position text where desired. Isn't it fun? You've just completed your first computer-generated or digital scrapbook page, and with a little experimentation, the sky is the limit to your digital creativity!

illustration J

Computer scrapbooking resources on the Internet

For the traditional scrapbooker who is toying with the idea of getting started in computer scrapbooking, there are hundreds of online communities and Web sites that can give you a "crash course" in digital scrapbooking.

Visit an online community or Web site to find tutorials on various techniques, add plug-ins and custom brushes to your creative repertoire and find ideas, insights and inspiration for creating your own paper backgrounds, fibers, page accents and more. You'll also find resourceful chat rooms or message boards for learning, as well as downloadable paper backgrounds, page accents, page kits and templates—designed by cutting-edge and innovative digital scrapbookers—to experiment with in your own image-editing software. Throughout the pages of this book, you'll also see sources for downloads and fonts listed in the Supplies lists of featured art. And don't forget to do an Internet search for free downloadable fonts and clip art, which are also valuable computer scrapbook page elements. Finally, among the many sites devoted to computer scrapbooking, you are sure to find a style to call your own—perhaps even a reflection of your traditional scrapbooking style.

These soft and sophisticated baby layouts were created by digital designer Doris Castle, who uses a variety of elements from downloaded PagePaks and AlphaSets found at CottageArts.net.

There are hundreds of Web sites devoted to computer scrapbooking. See what they have to offer to help you jumpstart your learning in this exciting and rapidly evolving scrapbook medium. Here are a few:

computerscrapbooking.com

cottagearts.net

digitaldesignessentials.com

digitalscrapbookdesign.com

digitalscrapbookplace.com

escrappers.com

esticker.com

gauchogirl.com

hp.com/scrapbooking

littlescrapper.com

pagesoftheheart.net

printlabseries.com

scrapbook-bytes.com

scrapbook-elements.com

scrapbookgraphics.com

scrappersguide.com

twopeasinabucket.com

Using digital downloads

There are many creative things you can do with downloaded digital kits and elements. They can be used "as is" by simply adding your photos, title and journaling with perfect coordination of color and style and you can use the elements however you wish. Or you can experiment with changing colors for a color-coordinated look to suit your computer-scrapbooking needs. With premade, downloaded page templates, add your photos, title and journaling for quick-and-easy computer scrapbooking. Perhaps the greatest benefit of downloaded elements is the fact that you can use them over and over again for a fresh new look every time!

What sweeter gift is there than a daughter who picks you flowers at every opportunity? Only one who also whispers "I love you" when she presents her special gifts.

July 2004

Digital Designer Tonya Doughty's page was created with elements from her custom collection Love Letters, which is available as a free download at www.gauchogirl.com/mms-bcomp.htm. The coordinated collection contains patterned papers, embellishments and an alphabet...already created in digital format for you to enhance or change as needed for your own layouts.

The digitalscrapbookplace.com's Margie Lundy created this fun tribute to a beloved bookcase and its contents using digital papers and elements from her Scraps of Life All About Me CD.

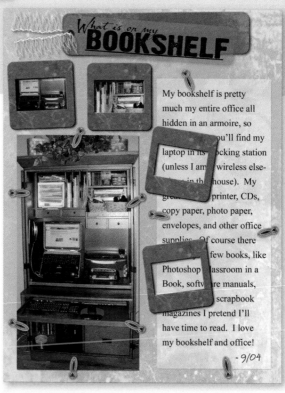

What is on my BOOKSHELF

My bookshelf is pretty much my entire office all hidden in an armoire, so ... you'll find my laptop in its ...cking station (unless I am... wireless else-... in th... house). My grea... printer, CDs, copy paper, photo paper, envelopes, and other office supplies. Of course there ... few books, like Photoshop ...assroom in a Book, softw...re manuals, ... scrapbook magazines I pretend I'll have time to read. I love my bookshelf and office!

-9/04

CONFUCIUS
SAY:

A smiling dog still
has his his teeth.
LUCKY NUMBERS: 3, 7, 8, 12, 29

WHERESOEVER
YOU GO,
GO WITH ALL
YOUR HEART.

Spring 2004

Creating Perfect Digital Paper & Paper Accents

One secret to stunning computer scrapbook pages is the background or "faux paper" foundation you start with. Spend some time playing around with your software and its functions to help you achieve the best results possible.

Image-editing and computer-scrapbooking software programs offer an endless array of backgrounds and colors to choose from. By experimenting with gradations, color saturation, opacity, brushes and filters, it's easy to achieve the precise style, pattern and texture you're looking for to help showcase your photographs.

Similar to a traditional scrapbook artist, as a computer scrapbooker you have a wide array of possibilities virtually at your fingertips for creating custom-made paper backgrounds and accents for a digital page. From simple color blocking and geometric shapes to translucent vellum and rough-hewn mulberry and canvas, you're just a few quick mouse clicks away from designing digital papers you will love.

Once you're comfortable designing your own papers, use the same techniques to create all the popular page accents—such as tags, slide mounts, library tabs, folders, paint chips and more. Use your scanner, too, to scan objects and images that can then be used as paper backgrounds and page accents for a truly custom look.

And don't forget about the wide array of downloadable "e-papers" and digital paper accents available on the Internet. They can be quick-and-easy solutions for the computer scrapbooker and can be easily customized to meet your page-design needs.

Single-color background

Create a clean and crisp scrapbook page with a single-color background, a black-and-white focal photo and colorful accent images. Traci tops off her dramatic page design with a combination of serif and script fonts for a showstopping look. Begin with a complementary-colored background. Crop, resize and layer photos on background. Finish with title in white.

Enjoy Life
Traci Turchin, Hampton, Virginia
Photo: Rice Photography, Lakebay, Washington

Supplies: Image-editing software (Adobe Photoshop CS); fonts (P22 Cezanne, Times New Roman)

Postage stamp sheet

Starting with a simple white background, Angela duplicates the look of a postage stamp sheet by using a round brush to draw dotted lines between her photos. To do this, select the brush type and size and then modify the spacing in the brush palette accordingly. Add sized photos. To create the virtual wax seal, experiment with different layer styles including bevel/emboss on a shape. Create little text boxes and rotate for "paper ribbons" beneath the wax seal. Elements such as the paw-print clip art become dimensional when you apply drop shadows or inner shadows to them.

Utah's Hogle Zoo

Angela M. Cable, Rock Springs, Wyoming

Supplies: Image-editing software (Jasc Paint Shop Pro 8); fonts (Arial, Garamond, P22 Monet); clip art (source unknown)

Color-blocking with depth

Shannon's clever use of color blocking and digital chalking brings depth and dimension her art while drawing the eyes straight in to the photos featured. Start with a color-blocked background. On a new layer, create several black, diagonal lines in varying widths with the Rectangular Shape tool at varying opacities. To "chalk" the lines, use the Spray Paint tool to spray color in varying shades along the edges of the lines, with darker paint applications towards the edges, then apply a Gaussian Blur effect to smooth the spray. Drag this layer onto background. Repeat this process for vertical lines in a complementary color on the lower half of the page. Add photos, title and journaling to complete the page.

The Makings of Peer Pressure

Shannon Freeman, Bellingham, Washington

Supplies: Image-editing software (Micrografx Draw 6.0, Microsoft Photo Editor, Microsoft Paint); fonts (Impact, Rockwell, Rockwell Bold)

You're going to win one-third of your games. It's the other third that makes the difference.

Color-block background

Simple pages are a great way to keep the emphasis on your photos. Here, Kristie used the colors from the pictures to create the background and accents. Using a canvas texture on your background layer is a very effective way of keeping your layout clean and simple while adding a more realistic feel to your page. This can be accomplished using the texturizer filter in your image-editing software. For the final touch, use simple rectangles and a dotted brush for your frames and title.

Baseball Love
Kristie L., Houston, Texas

Supplies: Image-editing software (Adobe Photoshop 7); fonts (CK Maternal, Pharmacy)

...*Baseball Love*.......... BOY MEETS BASEBALL

NO MATTER HOW GOOD YOU ARE, YOU'RE GOING TO LOSE ONE-THIRD OF YOUR GAMES. NO MATTER HOW BAD YOU ARE

Circle-shape background

Amy's pet photos pop right off the page when geometric shapes are used to create an eye-catching background. Draw circles with the shape tool onto colored background; apply emboss filter to create offset circles. Layer cropped and resized photos and complete with title and journaling.

The Many Moods of Mickey
Amy Trask, Marina, California
Photos: Carl Trask, Marina, California

Supplies: Image-editing software (Adobe Photoshop Elements); fonts (B52, Handprint, MA Sexy, Stamp Act)

The many MOODS of MICKEY

Oops!

Mickey has always been such a happy dog. He's proof that dogs can smile.

happy

Multishape background

When using digital papers and elements, it's always a good idea to experiment with drop shadows. Ronnie made good use of this technique by making her digital tags, eyelets and brads seem to float over the page rather than just lay flat on top. Try to use textures whenever possible and vary the angles of your backgrounds. When using so many papers and elements, try to keep the colors of your photo as neutral as possible, preferably grayscale or sepia.

Matter of Positioning
Ronnie McCray, St. James, Missouri

Supplies: Image-editing software (Adobe Photoshop Elements 2.0); fonts (2P's Flea Market; Bart, Beedley, Book Antiqua, Bradley Hand ITC, Butterbrotpapier)

Torn-paper background

By erasing with a brush, Andrea gave her page a torn look and allowed the colors on the bottom layer to pop out. To create this effect, select the eraser tool at 100-percent opacity and use a brush with interesting edges. After erasing on the top layer, be sure to add a drop shadow to get a more three-dimensional effect. You can also experiment erasing at different opacities.

Shootin' Hoops
Andrea Graves, Sandy, Utah

Supplies: Image-editing software (Adobe Photoshop 7); fonts (2P's Tasklist; Arial)

Patterned paper

By taking advantage of the many tools available in software programs, you can simulate realistic patterned paper pages and make your own papers right from your desktop. Elizabeth did this by creating a brush in Photoshop and then using it to make her "crumpled" paper. She also simulated torn paper and made it look even more realistic by adding a drop shadow. You can create endless options of papers and layer them on top of each other. Remember to add drop shadows for depth. When duplicating the look of a "traditional" page, don't make it look too perfect. Paper pages have a handmade look to them, and it's important to simulate this in your digital pages to get the right look.

Girly Girl
Elizabeth Lombardi, Yonkers, New York

Supplies: Image-editing software (Adobe Photoshop CS); fonts (JJStencil, MA Sexy, Hootie!, Marydale)

Punched paper

By using different hearts throughout, Valerie allows you to really feel the underlying message in this layout. Because the colors are bright, it is important to make your photos grayscale to avoid clashing. Use drop shadows to differentiate between your elements and layers. Such a varied repetition of patterns calls for a solid or at least muted journaling block. Using a brush to erase the edge between the heart paper and the photo allows for a smooth transition. The heart frame around the entire page brings it all together and draws your eye in to the center.

Sterling Always Sweet
Valerie Randall, Santa Rosa, California

Supplies: Image-editing software (Adobe Illustrator 10, Adobe Photoshop 7); fonts (Hootiel, Lucida Sans, Zothique)

Patterned paper from custom brushes

By using different shades and opacities of just two basic colors, Kristie has made a page that is soft and pleasing to the eye. You can create something similar, just be sure to select subtle colors and modify your photo to match them. Use aging brushes to give the page and your elements a weathered feel. Vary opacities and use brushes to "tear" pages. Use layer styles to create the metal look in the eyelets. If you're going to be adding this many items to one page, stick with one great photo. Kristie used many different programs to create this page, but if you don't have access to such a large variety, experiment with the different filter and editing options in your software. Remember, experimentation is the key to creating a page like this one.

Who Am I?

Kristie L., Houston, Texas
Photo: William L., Houston, Texas

Supplies: Image-editing software (Adobe Photoshop CS); filters (Auto FX Dreamsuite, Alien Skin Eye Candy 4000); fonts (2P's Sophisticated; Misproject, Pharmacy, Sketchby, St. Nicholas, Tangenne)

Vellum

Roseanne simulates the look of real vellum on her digital page using multiple layers and layer transparencies in her image-editing software. Achieve this look by layering numerous rectangle shapes and decreasing the opacity. Add a soft drop shadow. Polka dots or other shapes can be added between the layers to complete the look. You can create a tile background using a mosaic filter in image-editing software or you can purchase a program with specialty filters for more variety. Take advantage of some simple shapes and layer effects to draw your own elements like the bathtub on this page.

Rub-A-Dub

Roseanne Miske, Monument, Colorado

Supplies: Image-editing software (Adobe Photoshop CS, Alien Skin Xenofex2); font (Vitamin)

TANNER'S FIRST BIG POOL

Summer Fun

Patterned paper with crumpled texture

Use the Eyedropper tool to sample several colors from your main photo. These colors become the color palette for perfect coordination. Kristie used her own crumpled paper texture in cool blue to balance the vibrant yellow and also included light, bright green and tangerine in a striped paper ribbon accent to frame the main photo. A metallic circle element with repeated stripe background serves both as embellishment and punctuation to the title. DreamSuite Dreamy Photo filter creates the high-key photos and emphasizes the dreamlike quality of the layout.

Summer Fun
Kristie L., Houston, Texas

Supplies: Image-editing software (Adobe Photoshop 7); filters (Auto FX DreamSuite, Alien Skin Eye Candy 4000); fonts (scrapbookvillage.com's Pharmacy)

Word patterned paper

Rhonna's soft, custom-designed word papers work in unison with the blue tinting of her son's eyes to create the dreamy effect of her digital page. Working in layers, start with a background embellished with a circle brush. Create color blocks with various fonts, distress brush and frames or lines. Crop and resize photos. Use Magic Wand to select portion of black-and-white photos. Use the Eye Dropper to select color; fill in color and place photos on background. See Chapter 4 for instructions on how to make metal-rimmed tag and brads.

Love Those Eyes
Rhonna Farrer, Orem, Utah

Supplies: Image-editing software (Adobe Photoshop 7); fonts (dafont.com's Jet Plane, Kravitz, Migraine, True Golden); circle and distress brushes (artist's own designs)

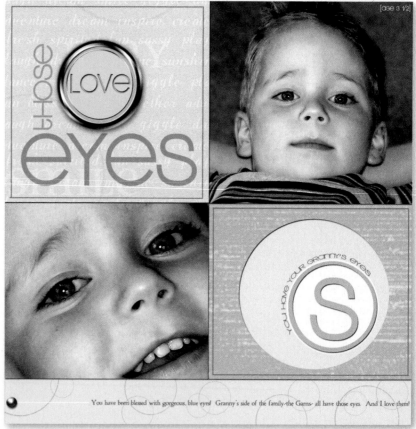

You have been blessed with gorgeous, blue eyes! Granny's side of the family-the Garns- all have those eyes. And I love them!

Mixing patterned papers

Veronica's four layouts exemplify a unique aspect of computer scrapbooking: You can use the same template over and over for consistency in page design. Or use the same template and completely change the look by simplying changing the paper colors and photo themes. Work in several layers to create one page, beginning with the background paper. Create various patterned papers by first creating custom brushes in your image-editing software. To create your own brush, start a new file. Draw the shape you want to convert to a brush or copy and paste a shape from another image. Select Edit > Define Brush, then name your brush and save it. Open the Brushes palette and select the new brush. Click and drag to create brushstrokes or place the cursor once to stamp the brush shape in place. Use Drop Shadows and the Bevel and Emboss tools to give the image a more realistic feel. Use your original photo as an embellishment in a lighter opacity. Choose a one-word title that describes each of her children's person-alities and duplicate the page for each child.

Smart, Snuggly, Spunky, Sweet
Veronica Ponce, Miami, Florida

Supplies: Image-editing software (Adobe Photoshop CS); fonts (Century Gothic; fontdiner.com's 4990810)

Patterned paper from clip art

Because blocking is a technique often used in traditional, paper-based scrapbooking, using a grid to create digital layouts lends a clean, realistic look. Use your software's ruler feature to ensure perfect alignment. Choose a complementary color and, using the grid, arrange a color-blocked area for the inspirational quote and as a border treatment to serve as background to a string of character words. Import photos and arrange to the grid. Use the same white as in the photos for the title block and text to help move the eye through the page. Leave the journaling block dark to anchor the layout and draw emphasis to the journaling.

Salt Lake City Marathon
Sande Krieger, Salt Lake City, Utah

Supplies: Image-editing software (Adobe Photoshop CS); brushes (Adobe Studio); fonts (Book Antique; Caeldera; Desdemona; CK's Carbon Copy, Constitution, Gutenberg, Typewriter, Vogue)

Patterned paper with shabby chic look

For this layout featuring several cruise photos, Sande chose blue as the background to represent the sea. The layered photos combined with white and monochromatic brushwork create the painted, collage look often seen in shabby chic layouts. Sande created brushes from fonts to stamp text and downloaded others resembling paint to lend authenticity.

Come Sail Away With Me
Sande Krieger, Salt Lake City, Utah

Supplies: Image-editing software (Adobe Photoshop CS); paintbrushes (Adobe Studio); text brushes (2P's Sailboat; Hannibal Lector); font (High Tower Text)

Patterned paper with realistic details

Taking the time to create several unique painted textures and stitching adds authenticity to this patriotic parade layout. Fill background with dark blue and use a "dry brush" brush to drag cream color down paper for whitewashed effect. Draw and repeat the cream star element. Additional brushwork on edges creates a painted-edge "grunge" look. Repeat technique for additional papers using vertical grain texture to create stripes, angle and layer as shown. Reduce opacity to create vellum. Create stitching with Picture Tubes or Brushes. Use custom shape to create paper clip, add metallic layer style and erase part of the clip to look realistically attached to photo. Attach a cutout copy of the star from the background paper and add a drop shadow for depth. Metal title and date art are fonts that have been enhanced with metallic layer styles.

Everyone Loves a Parade
Michelle Shefveland, Sauk Rapids, Minnesota

Supplies: Image-editing software (Adobe Photoshop Elements 2.0, Jasc Paint Shop Pro 8.1); fonts (Avril, Misproject, Punch Label); filters (Auto FX Mystical Lighting Effects)

DEPTH OF PERSONALITY

Your personality has many
LAYERS.
As you reveal each layer of
joy,

strength,

honesty,

perseverence,

stubborness,

and so many more...
I find how much
I love the real
YOU.

Downloaded paper altering

To place emphasis on her subject, a relatively small section of the photo, Doris framed it by creating a shadow box. Add drop shadow and emboss layer styles to create "box" then select rectangular areas with marquee tool and delete from shape to create depth. Monochromatic eyelets, also created using layer styles, add detail and serve to frame journaling. Add journaling and title in white for emphasis. Ghosted character words behind journaling add additional layers of depth.

Depth of Personality
Doris Castle, Fonda, New York

Supplies: Image-editing software, brushes (Adobe Photoshop); font (typadelic.com's Persimmon); background (cottagearts.net's Kids Valentine Page Pak by Doris Castle)

Patterned paper from shapes

Kristie uses her software's texture filters and brushes to create the background patterns for her papers. Her repeated soft color scheme ensures the papers all coordinate despite their differing patterns and help the grayscale photos to appear even more luminous. Convert photos to sepia and crop all the same size. Layer the papers and photos as shown and "attach" with staples (created with shapes and layer styles). Draw a rectangle using the marquee tool, fill with matching color and apply "leather." Create stitching using brushes and embossing layer styles. Make buckle with custom shapes and a metallic layer style. Erase small portion of leather straps where the buckle overlaps to look laced through buckle. Repeat stripe pattern as background to small metal frames stamped with text. Add title block and additional brushwork to create soft, grunge look to papers and elements.

Pure Innocence
Kristie L., Houston, Texas

Supplies: Image-editing software (Adobe Photoshop 7); leather filter (Alien Skin Eye Candy 4000); brushes (artist's own); fonts (dafont.com's McGarey, Porcelain; scrapvillage.com's Hootie!)

Metallic rivet paper

Fonda created a realistic background that mimics the riveted metal siding of the airplane in the photos. Create riveted aluminum background by making a circle and using layer styles to achieve metallic look. Use the Dodge/Burn tool to add discoloration and shading and repeat the rivets as shown. Additional page accents (propeller and gyroscope navigation instrument) were created using several custom shapes in layers to which brushes, Text and Layer Styles were applied to create realism. Title, journaling and stapled strip complete this high-flying layout.

North to Alaska
Fonda Darter, Slater, Iowa

Supplies: Image-editing software and brushes (Adobe Photoshop 7); fonts (typadelic.com's Moonbeam, Persimmon)

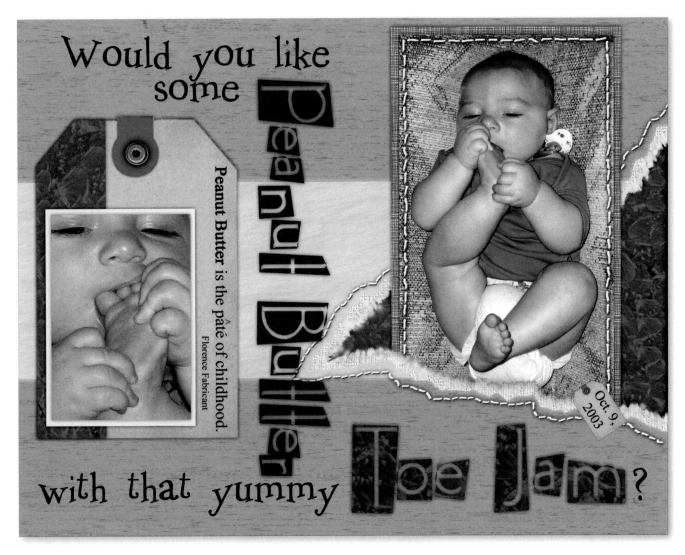

Stitching on page

For a fun themed background used to highlight the peanut butter and jam title, Ronnie created creamy brown and swirled purple papers using her software's texture files. Repeating the use of purple and brown in the title and tags play up the connection. The stitches are individual brush marks to which drop shadow and emboss layer styles have been added.

Peanut Butter & Toe Jam
Ronnie McCray, St. James, Missouri

Supplies: Image-editing software, brushes (Adobe Photoshop Elements 2.0, Microsoft Picture It! Photo 6.0);
fonts (2P's Flea Market, Field Marshal; Times New Roman)

Crumpled and textured paper

Roseanne used brushes and painted on several different layers to create the patterned paper. She flattened the layers to one, cropped it to be slightly smaller than her background and added a drop shadow to visually raise it above the solid colored cardstock background. A crumple filter was used to create the creased appearance. The ribbon is a rectangle of color to which a grosgrain-pattern layer effect was added. The ribbon is pinched using the liquefy or pinch filter, and a small section is duplicated above the buckle and then masked using a layer mask to look authentic as it passes through the buckle.

Always Bring Your Own Sunshine
Roseanne Miske, Monument, Colorado

Supplies: Image-editing software, brushes (Adobe Photoshop CS); filters (Alien Skin Xenofex2); fonts (Angelina, LainieDaySH)

Embossed vellum

When accentuating a special photo, it's often better to follow the "less is more" theory and help the portrait shine. Roseanne accomplishes this with subtle, serene color and elegant effects. Create embossed vellum using brushes and lowered opacity. Soften the edges using a deckle filter. To add a sheer ribbon, create the rectangle shape and lower the opacity. Create paths and use layer styles to "tie" the bow. A custom-shape heart colored to match the simple journaling becomes a charming accent and completes this gentle layout.

Of All the Things You Wear
Roseanne Miske, Monument, Colorado

Supplies: Image-editing software, brushes (Adobe Photoshop CS); filters (Auto FX Dream Suite); fonts (typadelic.com's Persimmon)

Aged papers

Tonya prefers not to rely solely on standard filter treatments to achieve texture, feeling they often lack the variety that real life brings. She uses filters on small, feathered portions of her papers over several layers and uses various blending modes to achieve better realism. She uses her software's drop shadow layer effect as a starting point and adds additional shadows and highlights by hand. Create additional texture by erasing small areas to age weathered and "gently handled" areas of paper and stamped or rubbed-on text.

Nature Girls
Tonya Doughty, Wenatchee, Washington

Supplies: Image-editing software (Adobe Photoshop CS); filters (Alien Skin Eye Candy 4000, Alien Skin Xenofex2); brushes (artist's own); fonts (dafont.com's Kingthings Printingkit; letteringdelights.com's Scrap Cursive); papers, elements (gauchogirl.com's Tres Jolie Kit by Tonya Doughty)

Mesh texture

For this colorful background, Mikki applied several of her program's built-in patterns to a layer filled with color. Using layer masks allowed her to alter the way the patterns affected the background. She converted the photos to sepia tone and then faded the effect to allow some of the natural colors to show through. A mesh eyelet anchors the photo in the left-hand corner.

Fall

Mikki Livanos, Jacksonville, Florida

Supplies: Image-editing software (Adobe Photoshop 7); fonts (CK's Cursive; Perpetua)

Cross-stitch canvas

Susan began her layout by filling a background shape with white and using a patchwork filter to create the Aida cross-stitch fabric. A rose-colored rectangle is cut out and serves as a journaling block. She drop-shadowed the text to make it "pop," and two embossed cross shapes serve as both anchors and embellishment. Complete the layout by framing with a beveled and embossed mat in soft lavender.

Mirror, Mirror on the Wall

Susan Steffens, DeWitt, Michigan

Supplies: Image-editing software (Microsoft Digital Image Pro 9); filters (Alien Skin Eye Candy 4000, Alien Skin Splat!); fonts (Monotype Corsiva, Wendy Medium)

Embossed paper

We're all used to using tools to scrapbook our photos, but what about using photos as tools? Ronnie uses interesting photos to create unique textures for her papers. For the background shown here, she opened a photo comprised of a swirl of marbled colors. She then saved this as a .PSD (Photoshop) file into her Photoshop Elements textures folder. She filled her paper with stripes of color and then ran the texture filter using the .PSD file she saved in the previous step. The height of the texture is created based on the lightness and darkness of the file used. To complete her layout, Ronnie added subtle script journaling and a faux filmstrip created by cutting squares out of a long rectangle and adding shadows.

James Sleep
Ronnie McCray, St. James, Missouri

Supplies: Image-editing software (Adobe Photoshop Elements 2.0); fonts (Hannibal Lector, Texas Hero, Times New Roman)

Leather texture

One technique for creating coordinated layouts is to carry the theme of the photos past the border and out into the page. Ronnie does this by making a realistic football leather texture that serves as both background and embellishment. Using the eyedropper tool to get the exact color, she drew and filled a square and then used a football texture filter compatible with her program. The pebbled surface ads its own depth and dimension and anchors the photos and other elements to perfectly capture this rugged, athletic memory.

Football Player Wannabe
Ronnie McCray, St. James, Missouri

Supplies: Image-editing software (Adobe Photoshop Elements 2.0); fonts (Cooper, Hannibal Lector, Times New Roman)

With no school Carsey turned into a night owl over the summer.

August 2004

Painted canvas

Because the photos in her layout were taken at night and have little natural light of their own, Tonya wanted her papers to have a luminous glow. Using a lot of brushwork, build up layers of color washes of varying opacity and use various blending modes to control the way they interact with layers below. Mask out circles from some of the colors to form the moon shape to match the nighttime theme. Photos and a tag are attached with coordinated eyelets and the journaling is made to appear stamped over the edge of the paper. After creating the title letters, load the selection, contract it and stroke the path with an X-shaped brush. The series of Xs are embossed to look like cross-stitches. Finally, create a duplicate set of letters, slightly enlarged and colored black, to serve as a layered mat for the colored portion. The stitches appear to join the two. She added additional shadowing by hand to achieve a realistic look.

From Dusk 'til Dawn
Tonya Doughty, Wenatchee, Washington

Supplies: Image-editing software (Adobe Photoshop CS); brushes (artist's own); fonts (dafont.com's Kingthings Printingkit; letteringdelights.com's LD Letterpress); papers, elements (gauchogirl.com's Barfly Kit by Tonya Doughty)

Rough-hewn mulberry paper

Colleen wanted to highlight the unique colors of the carousel horses and lights in this photo of her son's first ride. She used the color sampler tool to select several of the colors and applied them to various paper layers. To achieve the torn look for the papers, she used the Distort/Displace filter with horizontal and vertical scales both set to 20 percent. The displacement map used was a photo she took of crushed shale from her backyard. Standard Photoshop texture filters gave the paper a handmade quality. Finally, each paper was drop-shadowed to look layered. Colleen then added journaling and a title that she "debossed" so as to appear cut out of the paper.

Carousel
Colleen Yoshida, Cold Lake, Alberta, Canada

Supplies: Image-editing software (Adobe Photoshop 7)

Carousel

When we saw the carousel on the pier in Seattle we weren't sure how you would like it but decided to take a shot anyway. I put you on the horse, and as soon as the carousel started, so did the giggling. You held on to the bar and laughed, giggled and smiled the whole time the horse was moving. When I went to take you off the horse, you even started crying to get back on!

Ethan in Seattle July 2004

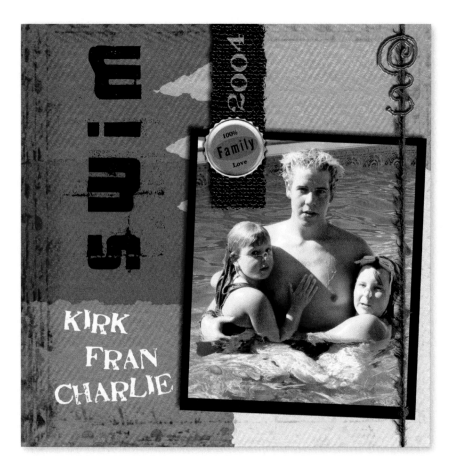

Denim paper

When a challenge was issued to use art as inspiration, Wendy jumped on board with a piece titled "Conscientiousness II" by John Palmer. She was inspired by the clean color blocking aspect of the art and re-created several of the key color placements for her layout. She drew blocks of each color, applied the Xenofex Distress filter to get the ragged edges and then arranged to her liking. To create the distressed edge around the layout, she used various eraser shapes and opacities to erase along the edge while using assorted colors. Adding a denim texture completes her background. Her sparing use of embellishment—just a bottle cap, twill tape, fiber and metal clip—emphasizes the modern, clean feel to her page.

Swim

Wendy Gibson, Mission, British Columbia, Canada

Supplies: Image-editing software (Corel Photopaint 8); filters (Alien Skin Eye Candy 4000, Flaming Pear Blade Pro); fonts (Stamp Act)

Bleached photo paper

Angela admits to probably having too many pictures of her cat, C.C., but this quote from her collection of cat quotes fit the photo so well she had to scrap it. She created the textured paper background and tore the edge, which serves to both embellish the layout and emphasize the quote. The photo is repeated as a ghosted monochromatic image and decorated with the subtle, digitally "bleached" letters of her cat's name to echo the graceful theme. Black label tape nicknames visually balance and complete the layout.

Graceful

Angela M. Cable, Rock Springs, Wyoming

Supplies: Image-editing software (Jasc Paint Shop Pro 8); fonts (A Yummy Apology, GF Ordner, Studio Script)

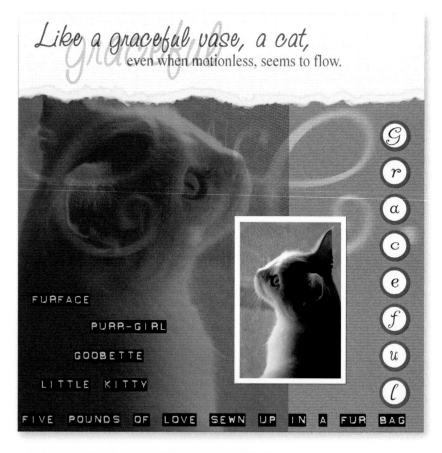

Distressed and stitched photo paper

When Penny wanted to create a layout tailored exactly to the subject of the photo, she decided to "get personal." Using a cropped section of the face of her dog, Belle, she created a custom fill pattern which, when muted a soft blue, became a totally custom background. Another portion of the background is filled with words that remind Penny of Belle and her importance to the family. Silver accents include brads, a paw print and a dog bone bearing Belle's name. Bone-stamped paper, a monochromatic color palette and zigzag stitching complete this doggone lovable layout.

Doggone Lovable
Penny Dutcher, Denver, Colorado

Supplies: Image-editing software (Photoshop 7); fonts (2P's Sunflower, Arial Black, Beths Cute HMK Bold, Broadway BT, Crack Babies)

Canvas photo paper

Sande's inspiration for this layout was the serene, tourist-less Venice she saw in the early morning before most people were awake. For each side of this two-page layout, she chose one of her favorite photos and created a subtle, textured, monochromatic background. The remaining photos repeat the sepia tone, and the elegant, airy title and quote blend seamlessly to complete this layout evocative of another time and place.

Venezia Italia
Sande Krieger, Salt Lake City, Utah

Supplies: Image-editing software (Adobe Photoshop CS); fonts (Kimzler Script, Maranda GD, Pepita MT, Papyrus)

Slide mounts and library tab

To emphasize the main photo, Rachel centered it on a simple white background with only a drop shadow and single red poemstone for adornment. To balance the layout, she reversed the opposite side to black and drew a red ribbon on which she placed three high-contrast duplicates of the photo. Her heartfelt journaled poem underscores the tender photo and serves to soften the dramatic black and white.

A Child to Hold And Cuddle

Rachel Dickson, Calgary, Alberta, Canada

Supplies: Image-editing software (Adobe Photoshop CS); font (Century)

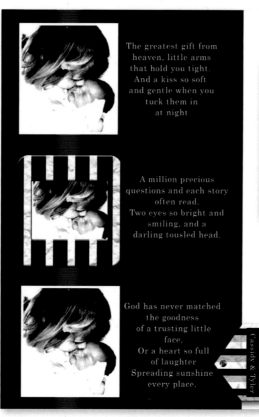

The greatest gift from heaven, little arms that hold you tight. And a kiss so soft and gentle when you tuck them in at night

A million precious questions and each story often read. Two eyes so bright and smiling, and a darling tousled head.

God has never matched the goodness of a trusting little face, Or a heart so full of laughter Spreading sunshine every place.

A child to **hold** and **cuddle**, is a **gift** from God above, And the world is so much **brighter** When you have a child to **love**.

Manila folder pocket

Rachel duplicates a common paper scrapbooking technique to bring authenticity to her digital layout. First create a file folder with both a front and back, sandwiching a photo in between, and then create shadowing for a realistic look. Her other layered effects—a stamped ribbon, torn paper, matted photo and photo turns—combine for a three-dimensional layout that is anything but flat!

Attitude

Rachel Dickson, Calgary, Alberta, Canada

Supplies: Image-editing software (Adobe Photoshop CS); fonts (Book Antiqua, Crack Babies, Problem Secretary)

The position of the body and limbs A manner of acting. A relatively stable and enduring predisposition to behave or react in a characteristic way.

(at·ti·tude)

Attitude

Aa

Tags

The beautiful brown palette in Ronnie's photos is repeated in her layout to create a strong masculine page. She uses several shades in a striped background, created by drawing an elongated rectangle and duplicating across a colored background. The vertical stripes help balance the strong horizontal nature of the page. The stitched accent stripe is created by using a brush to draw strokes and then applying a bevel and emboss filter. Stretching the title and subtitle across the main photo and onto the right side of the page ties the layout together and the journaling tag tells the story of the layout.

Trouble Is Brewing
Ronnie McCray, St. James, Missouri

Supplies: Image-editing software (Adobe Photoshop Elements 2.0); fonts (Cheltpress Trial, John Handy LET, Stamp Act, Times New Roman)

Paint chips

Many paper embellishments can be created digitally and have the added benefit of being customizable. Here, Rachel created paint sample strips like those at the hardware store and then matched them perfectly to her sepia-toned photo and mostly monochromatic page. A poemstone, silver photo corners, metal accent word and stencil letters are all traditional paper scrapbook elements translated beautifully to this entirely digital layout. She adds subtle distressed papers in the background and digital stitching to complete without taking focus away from the photo.

My Baby Boy
Rachel Dickson, Calgary, Alberta, Canada

Supplies: Image-editing software (Adobe Photoshop CS); fonts (Century, Impact, Stencil)

I get kissed by the sun each morning
Put my feet on a hardwood floor
I get to hear my children laughing
Down the hall through the bedroom door
Sometimes I sit on my front porch swing
Just soakin' up the day
I think to myself, I think to myself
This world is a beautiful place

I have been blessed
And I feel like I've found my way
I thank God for all I've been given
At the end of every day
I have been blessed
With so much more than I deserve
To be here with the ones that love me
To love them so much it hurts
I have been blessed

Across a crowded room
I know you know what I'm thinking
By the way I look at you
And when we're lying in the quiet
And no words have to be said
I think to myself, I think to myself
This love is a beautiful gift

I am so blessed
And I feel like I've found my way
I thank God for all I've been given
At the end of every day
I have been blessed
With so much more than I deserve
To be here with the ones that love me
To love them so much it hurts
I have been blessed

When I'm singin' my kids to sleep
When I feel you holdin' me
I know
I am so blessed...
                        - Sung by Martina McBride

BLESSED

Photo Manipulation Made Easy

2

One of the most fun yet challenging aspects of computer scrapbooking is photo manipulation. With a click of the mouse you can transform a image into a clever piece of digital photo art. Or combine several images and manipulation techniques to design a true masterpiece.

Experiment, experiment, experiment! It's the fastest way to learn about your software's capabilities. The more familiar you are with your image-editing software, the more enjoyable photo manipulation will be. Take advantage of the software's onscreen help tutorials or user manual. Explore the software's features on just one photo, practicing simple things like resizing and cropping images. Then explore with adjustments to sharpness and brightness/contrast or hue/saturation. With each tool or filter you apply, note how the image is transformed. Undo each adjustment and

move on to the next adjustment. When you feel comfortable with basic photo manipulation, begin working in layers. Try adding text to an image. Experiment with artistic filter effects to make your photo look like a watercolor painting, perhaps. Apply and undo every possible color and filter adjustment, exploring all of the options your software offers to ensure endless creative possibilities with little to no effort.

Start with simple page designs and progress to more advanced layouts. And if you don't like a certain adjustment or effect, you can delete or undo the layer and try something new.

In no time at all, you'll be creating stunning collages, photomontages and visually appealing computer scrapbook pages. An entire world of photo creativity and expressive personal style awaits you.

Simple cropping

Shannon crops images from backgrounds and replaces them with new background textures for a bright and clean look. Choose a good main action shot for the central image, convert its background layer to a new layer or cut out image and use the eraser tool to remove the excess background effectively cutting out the subject. Place another photo such as a wood texture on a layer behind the subject so it is the new background. Create the photo at the top of the page in a similar manner and use the saturation tool to de-saturate the cutout image removing its color. Place a photo of sky behind this photo and increase the color saturation of the sky with the saturation tool. Use part of this sky image at the foot of the page as a background for the title text.

Aspirations

Shannon L. Freeman, Bellingham, Washington

Supplies: Image-editing software (Micrografx Draw 6.0, Microsoft Paint); fonts (2P's Hot Chocolate; CK's Newsprint)

Shape cropping

Use the pre-designed shapes that come with your scrapbook or image-editing software to add character to photos. To expound further on her photos' theme, MaryJo cleverly used her own hand-drawn clip-art petroglyphs for a custom background. First, select a color for background; scan, size and place clip art on background shaded at 20 percent. Select a photo shape and crop photos. Size photos and layer with the same shape in black for a faux mat. Add title and journaling to complete page.

Manitou Cliff Dwellings

MaryJo Regier, Memory Makers Books

Supplies: Page-design software (HP's Creative Scrapbook Assistant); clip art (artist's own design)

Silhouette cropping

Helen ensures this photo has sufficient black around it so it looks as if it is cut from its background. Shoot your photo with a dark or black background and, if necessary, do as Helen did and use the clone stamp tool to sample and paint the black areas from the photo over any extraneous background so it is all black leaving just the central figure. Create a page border of red and add snowflakes using a snowflake font. Finish with a title and date.

Joy

Helen Shi-Yuen, Lawrenceville, New Jersey

Supplies: Image-editing software (Adobe Photoshop); fonts (Bell, dafont.com's WWFlakes)

Silhouette cropping

Angel turns a so-so shot of her little boy Ruhl holding a ball and fresh from the bath into a compelling scrapbook page with a fun message. Start by masking the background of a photo leaving just the child and the ball and replace the background part black and part blue. Use the lens flare filter to make the stars on the black part of the background. Mask the ball and replace it with a clip-art photo of the earth sized to the same size as the ball. Add shading along the bottom of the globe and the child's hands in the same places that the shading appears on the original ball so it appears as if the earth is actually held in the child's hands. Finish with a title and journaling.

This Is My World

Angel Richards, Kennesaw, Georgia

Supplies: Image-editing software (Adobe Photoshop 7); fonts (2P'sTypo; dafont.com's Stamp Act freeware font by Harold's fonts)

Silhouette cropping

Carrie rescues this humorous photo of her son using a cropped and spotlighted effect. Clean up the photo using the clone-stamp tool to remove unwanted elements and reflections. Use the magnetic lasso tool to trace around the subject and cut and paste the selection to a new layer. Select the background layer and apply a lighting effects filter using Filter > Render > Lighting Effects and use the Flashlight and Omni settings. Merge the layers back again. Create the circular picture frames and ribbon using custom shapes and fill edges with desired colors. Apply a texture to the ribbon to achieve a ribbed look. Crop three additional photos and place on the frames and size to fit. Add text on various layers using different colors and layer opacities. Use the text warp tool to manipulate the text such as for the word Smile and to bend text around the circular frames.

You Make Me Smile
Carrie Stephens, Leamington, Ontario, Canada

Supplies: Image-editing software (Adobe Photoshop CS); fonts (source unknown)

Photo tearing

Margie's trip to Seven Caves prompted this rugged design using torn photos, burlap and etched letters. Create a torn photo look using the Lasso tool to select a rough edge and delete it, then use the image invert tool to make the edge white. Use the noise filter to add digital noise to the edge to roughen it. Assemble images in layers over a plain background color and roughly brush on the background with a darker paint color to make it appear sanded. For the burlap layer, create a filled shape and apply a weave texture to it and a color overlay. Use the Little Days font in silver color for the look of twisted wire letters and add a bevel and drop shadow to suggest dimension. For the metal letters, cut out various shapes from a silver layer and add noise using the noise filter. Add a bevel and emboss layer style and a drop shadow for dimension. Type a letter over each metal shape and apply a reverse bevel to each letter. To make photos and burlap look dimensional, move parts of some layers behind others and add drop shadows to the edges of objects that appear over others ensuring the shadows appear on the same edges of all objects to reflect a single strong light source.

Seven Caves
Margie Lundy, Greenfield, Ohio

Supplies: Image-editing software (Adobe Photoshop 7); fonts (misprintedtype.com's Shortcut; Times New Roman; westwindfonts.com's Little Days)

Photo mosaic

Dana uses a photo mosaic effect to make this photo of the National Cathedral in Washington, D.C. look like it has been taken through a large window. Open the photo and use the marquee tool to select large vertical rectangles from the photo. Copy them to a second file leaving spaces between each strip for the vertical lines in the mosaic. Merge all layers and repeat the process this time selecting horizontal-shaped rectangles. Merge the layers and add a soft Bevel to all the photo squares. Add a black background behind the photo and complete the page with your title and journaling on a new top layer.

Serene
Dana Zarling, Middleton, Wisconsin

Supplies: Image-editing software (Adobe Photoshop 7); fonts (CK's Cursive; Times New Roman)

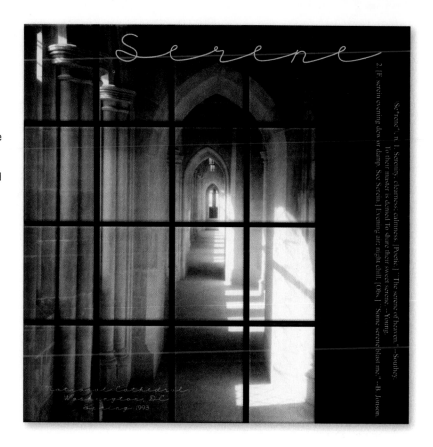

Photo kaleidoscope

Jeanie creates a photo kaleidoscope as a frame for this cute photo. Start in the Kaleidoscope Kreator and create your kaleidoscope image the size required for your page. In your image-editing software fill the page background with a texture pattern and duplicate the background layer. Use the lighting effects filter with the texture channel set to an alpha channel containing the title text. Make a duplicate of the background texture, delete all but a narrow border around the outer edge and apply a bevel and emboss layer style for the page border. Copy the kaleidoscope image minus its background onto the page and center it. Make a selection around the kaleidoscope and, on a new layer, stroke along the selection and fill the stroke with the background pattern then apply the bevel and emboss styles. Add another photo to the center of the kaleidoscope positioning it under the stroke layer and use a layer mask on the stroke layer to remove the portion covering the fingers. Create a cutout from a third photo and position the photo so it looks like the child is holding up the kaleidoscope. Duplicate and flip this layer so there is a child on both sides. Create a soft shadow under the child's feet. Finish by making a rectangular selection under the kaleidoscope, copying it to a new layer and applying a motion blur for a brushed metal effect. Add a bevel, digital brads and text.

Peek-a-Boo
Jeanie Sumrall-Ajero for Kaleidoscope Collections, Fort Collins, Colorado

Supplies: Kaleidoscope Kreator (Kaleidoscope Collections); image-editing software (Adobe Photoshop 7); fonts (1001font.com's Boyz R Gross; Copperplate Gothic Bold)

Basic photo collage

Melissa creates this handsome page using a series of similar photos for the bottom and middle photo collages. Begin by copying four photos to the bottom third of your page layout and use a layer mask to merge them. Place the photos over the background color and set the opacity to 40 and the fill to 70. Create the middle montage using three photos cropped to the same size. Apply filters and corrections as required to make the colors and contrast match. Under the photos place pieces of grass cut from the original photos to create a background and fill the gaps and repeat for the trees—aim for coverage and don't worry too much about making it look exactly seamless. Add color to the top of the page, two horizontal lines and your text and title.

Splendor In The Grass
Melissa Squires, Tecumseh, Michigan

Supplies: Image-editing software (Adobe Photoshop CS); font (font.com's Carpenter)

Motion blur for illusion of movement

Veronica successfully makes action shots of her son appear to fly into this page's foreground. Begin with a main action shot in the bottom layer, keeping photo at full opacity. While this image appears to be on top of the others, it's actually on the bottom layer since its background will be used for the other images as well. Adjust the levels so that the background is almost completely white. Use the Hue/Saturation feature to saturate specific colors in the photo, such as the yellow and blue in the child's clothing. Duplicate image and completely erase the background; add a motion blur to this second image layer and decrease opacity to 50 percent. Duplicate the second image layer, add motion blur and decrease layer opacity to 20 percent for the third image layer. Add a coordinating image in the upper left corner as far away from the motion as possible to avoid detraction from layered images. Use color balance, Hue/Saturation or a Gaussian-Blur filter to blend new image with the layered photos. Add title, saying and date journaling to the page in a simple font, using a more dramatic font for the words you want to emphasize. Experiment with the opacity on the text layers for a different look or pick up color from the photos with the eyedropper tool to create a coordinating color block for the layout, keeping the page as clean and crisp as possible.

He Who Would Learn to Fly
Veronica Ponce, Miami, Florida

Supplies: Image-editing software (Adobe Photoshop CS); fonts (Chisel, Century Gothic, Staccatto 222)

Monochromatic photo collage

Penny makes her own coordinating background using a blue flower in the same tones as her daughter's ballet dress. Open a photo of a blue flower in the tiling program 20/20 and create a tiled background. Add this to your page file and apply the fresco artistic effect to it. Copy this layer and at random select colors at different tolerances and delete them to get a patchy look. Decrease this layer's opacity. Use two photos of the same subject and select around the subject, invert the selection and delete the background. Finish with the eraser and remove any remaining unwanted edges. Copy the main photo and add it to the layout. Colorize it blue using the hue tool and adjust its layer opacity to make it partially transparent. Add the second image at a smaller size with a reduced opacity. Add the main image again, this time at full opacity. Finish with text and partially transparent shapes filled with colors sampled from the image.

Beautiful Ballerina
Penny Dutcher, Denver, Colorado
Photos: Cheri Tababa of Zemi Photographics, Denver, Colorado

Supplies: Image-editing software (20/20, Adobe Photoshop 7); filter (Alien Skin Eye Candy 4000); fonts (2P's Harlequin, Plain Jane, Pancake; International Palms; Kravitz; Wingdings)

Photo collage with inset

Michelle uses a colorful and soft-focused photo to draw attention to the main photo. Create the artistic photo edge for the lower right photo in Photoshop Elements 2.0 by erasing with a standard wet media brush. Add painting effects and a custom soft focus effect to the background wedding cake photo in Paint Shop Pro, and give it a crackle finish with AutoFX Dream Suite 1. Assemble the background photo and smaller photo into one document and adjust the opacity of the small photo to 85 percent to blend it into the background. Add word art using a new layer over both images and set the blend mode of overlay to create a luminous effect. Add the title and journaling using the same overlay blend mode.

Reflection of My Soul
Michelle Shefveland, Sauk Rapids, Minnesota

Supplies: Image-editing software (Adobe Photoshop Elements 2.0, Auto FX Dream Suite 1, Jasc Paint Shop Pro 8.1); fonts (Codex Text; myfonts.com's P22 Cezanne)

Photo collage from series

Laura Lee's page is a Christmas gift for her girlfriend and features a series of photos of her girlfriend and her sister as children. The photos are arranged "collage style" and the journaling is a poem specially written by Laura Lee. Scan old photos from a series of photos taken at the same time and correct the color in them, if necessary. Use the marquee tool with a very large feather value to select around each of the photos and copy each photo to a new layer in your page file. Use a soft eraser to blend the photos together. Create the background using a color sampled from one of the photos and then brush over it with a plaidlike brush varying the size and opacity as you brush over the background and the edges of the photos to create texture. Layer the word "Sister" typed in various fonts over the background using a very low opacity setting so the text is very faint. Add a poem or journaling to complete the layout.

Sisters
Laura Lee Shirt, Sherwood Park, Alberta, Canada

Supplies: Image-editing software (Adobe Photoshop 7); fonts (flyerstarter.com's Blackjack; Papyrus, Scriptina)

Photo collage with geometrics

Amy uses simple frames to draw attention to the main image in her photo collage. Start with a new file with a green background and add the photo onto a new layer. Make duplicates of this layer and move the layers so the photos are staggered over the page. Reduce the opacity of the photo layers using a different setting for each and leave the main image at near full opacity. In a new file make a frame using the pencil tool and, when you're satisfied with its shape, drag it onto the page. Make a copy of this layer and rotate it, add layer styles to the un-rotated frame to enhance it and give it a drop shadow. Use various brushes (Amy used brushes from Insomniac and Truly Sarah) to enhance the collage look. Finish with a title and journaling.

Pure Joy
Amy Dalrymple, Zanesville, Ohio

Supplies: Image-editing software (Adobe Photoshop Elements 2.0); brushes (Insomniac, Truly-Sarah); fonts (dafont.com's Lainie Day; Rough Typewriter)

Tinted photos

Melyssa added wings and fairy dust to her son's photo for a whimsical touch. Start with a photo of a child, duplicate the photo layer and convert this layer to black and white using Image > Adjust > De-saturate. Use the brush to draw outline and black lines of wings on a new layer. Select the spaces in the wings and fill with color using the Gradient fill tool. Reduce the layer opacity to 50 percent and use Filter > Blur > Gaussian to blur the wings. Make a selection around the wings and remove the detail from this area on the photos. Add a soft drop shadow to the wings. Select the black-and-white photo layer and, with the Eraser tool, erase the blue jeans exposing the color from the layer underneath. On the color layer, use the Color Range tool to select the darkest blue in the jeans, copy this selection to a new layer and apply a Gaussian Blur. Repeat with a selection of the lightest shade of blue from the jeans. Create the fairy dust with a 6- or 8-point star brush-tip shape setting the size jitter to 75 percent and the angle jitter to 33 percent in the shape dynamics and the scatter 156 percent and the count to 3 in the scatter options. Use a white foreground color and a new layer and paint stars from the child's hand to the ground. Flatten the image and, with the oval marquee, select around the image, invert the selection and apply a Gaussian Blur before adding the photo to the page.

Magical
Melyssa Connolly, Truro, Nova Scotia, Canada

Supplies: Image-editing software (Adobe Photoshop7); fonts (Arial, Scriptina)

every moment with you is *Magical*

Tinted photos

Roseanne creates the look of a hand-tinted photo with a simple painting technique. Make a duplicate of the background layer of the main photo and make the top layer black-and-white by using the de-saturate adjustment to reduce the color saturation. Use the history brush on the top layer to paint back the color from the original photo underneath in the areas you want colored. To create the acryliclike hearts, create a basic heart shape using custom shapes and create a layer style using the Drop Shadow > Satin > Inner Glow > Outer Glow > Bevel and Emboss > Inner Shadow options. Create the title and then rasterize the type layer; fill each block with a solid pink color. Add a Drop Shadow to letters so they resemble stickers.

Our Little Beauty
Roseanne Miske, Monument, Colorado

Supplies: Image-editing software (Adobe Photoshop CS); fonts (2P's Sugar-plums, Gingersnap)

I dreamed of a wedding

of elaborate elegance,

a church filled with family

and friends. I asked him

what kind of a wedding

he wished for, he said one

that would make me his wife.

Distressed photos

Angela's inspiration for this page is from a greeting card. Alter the photo's tone to sepia style by first de-saturating the photo then use the black-and-white points adjustment and select the sepia preset, or select your own option for the grey tone so you achieve the overall tonal change to the photo that you want. Select Layers > Load/Save Mask > Load Mask From Disk and choose a mask to apply to the photo to distress its edges. Create the actual page file with a white background and copy the photo to a new layer in it. Use the Deformation tool to skew the photo to a pleasing angle. Apply chalking to a new layer with a brush configured with your choice of pink color and set the brush to a low density and hardness value, high opacity and middle range step value. Save brushes like this to use another time. Finish by adding simple text elements to the page so they don't compete with the photo for attention.

Wedding Day
Angela M. Cable, Rock Springs, Wyoming

Supplies: Image-editing software (Jasc Paint Shop Pro 8); fonts (Carpenter IGG, Garamond)

Blended and distressed photos

Stacy distresses the edges of her photos to blend them into the page background. Start with a patterned background and add your photos in layers over this. Distress all the photos using a mask layer and erasing their edges to display the background underneath. On the main photo layer, brush the edges of the photo to create inklike look. Duplicate the smaller photos and de-saturate the topmost version of each image then adjust the brightness, contrast and levels and colorize each of them. Reduce the layer opacity to 80 percent so the original color shows through the tinted image. Add journaling around the edges of the small photos. Create a large floral brush from a photo and use this and other brushes to further distress the paper and pictures.

Family Adventure
Stacy Fox-Myers, Fremont, California

Supplies: Image-editing software (Adobe Photoshop Elements 2.0); fonts (Base 02, Migraine Serif, Pharmacy, Times and Times Again); brushes (misprintedtype.com; ti-fi.com/digitalbristle)

Sepia-antiqued photos

Jill's design captures the old look of the historical park she visited and her daughter's reaction to the music there. Start with a background layer filled with a tan color. Use four photos, de-saturate them and copy them into position on the layout placing three in the top left corner and one in the bottom right corner. Link the layers and set the layer blend mode to color burn. Duplicate this layer, change the blend mode to luminosity and lower the opacity to 30 percent to lighten them. Add a fifth photo to the bottom left corner setting its layer blend mode to luminosity and add a filled brown rectangle on a layer behind it to boost its color. Add a narrow white rectangle down the page for the title and reduce its opacity. Type the title text in brown and set the layer blend mode to linear burn. Add journaling to the top right corner with a brown shape behind it to boost its color. Jill finishes with custom-made brushes over the text box to age it and then applies these over the layout to scratch it to complete the aged effect.

Shake Your Booty
Jill Caren, Matawan, New Jersey

Supplies: Image-editing software (Adobe Photoshop CS); fonts (Arial, dafont.com's Metallic Avocado)

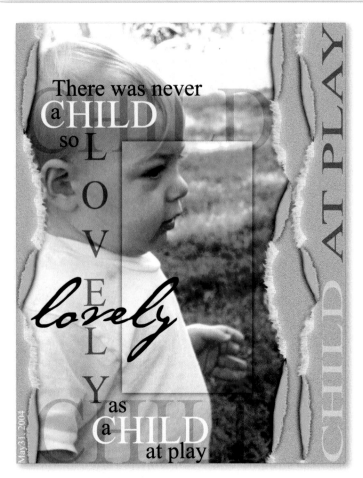

De-saturated color-photo

Ronnie creates this wonderful page with saturated and de-saturated layers and a single photo. Add the photo to the page and duplicate it. Convert the bottom photo layer to sepia using a filter. Select around the area to leave colored on the top layer and crop the remainder of the layer before applying a drop shadow to the layer. Roll the edges on the right border by drawing the rolled edges and then using the paintbrush to draw in the shadows. Use the Lasso tool to create jagged edges and add a white layer underneath to resemble torn edges. Again, with the Lasso tool, create jagged edges and add texture and drop shadow for dimension to mimic rolled edges. Finish with layers of words at different sizes and opacities.

Child at Play
Ronnie McCray, St James, Missouri

Supplies: Image-editing software (Adobe Photoshop Elements 2.0); fonts (Hannibal Lector, Times New Roman)

Layered shades of same photo

Janice uses layers, including multiples of the same photo, to create this attention-getting layout. Create the background by layering geometric shapes overlaid with layers of brushwork at varying opacity levels and using different colors. Outline selected shapes with a stroke line and add a bevel for dimension. Create the sun using a custom shape and apply a shadow and outer glow to it. Add the photo to a new layer and duplicate the layer. Reduce the opacity of one photo layer so the background is visible through it. Make second photo a duo tone before importing it: Image > Mode > Grayscale > Duo Tone. Transform the perspective on this photo layer so it appears to be twisting away.

Shy
Janice Dye-Szucs, Oshawa, Ontario, Canada

Supplies: Image-editing software (Adobe Photoshop); fonts (CK's Twilight; typadelic.com's Sweet Pea)

A sun this brilliant could not be hidden behind a cloud of bashfulness

Spot-de-saturated photos

Tracy uses a mix of color and sepia in the one photo in this attractive layout. Duplicate your photo, leaving the bottom photo layer untouched, and convert the top layer to sepia tone. Use the eraser tool on the top layer to remove the sky letting the blue color from underneath show through. Create a paint wash effect for the border using a brush and white color at a mid-level opacity. To apply chalk over this, use a brown color and brush it on at various opacities to get a rough finish. Finish with a title and, for the journaling, sample a color from the sky for the type. Add a digitally created eyelet, metal bead chain and tag.

Moment

Tracy Watson, Hallett Cove, South Australia, Australia

Supplies: Image-editing software (Adobe Photoshop); fonts (Applescruffs, Bambino)

Photo as background

Work first on your background papers and then add the images. In this case, Veronica used different brushes in different layers to create the background. Although each brush was painted in the same, or very similar, color, layer modes and varying opacities created the contrasts. Place the final papers on one layer and then add your photos. When working with duotone pages, use white or black as your highlight color. Vary the grayscale tonalities in your photos by increasing or decreasing the levels. Here, the larger photo was lightened significantly and the photo was placed to look like Savannah was walking off the page. Keep your sequence shots together and line them up to show the series. These can be outlined with a color block to separate them from the background. Two-page spreads are a great way to spread out a series of photos and give you one key accent page and another storytelling page.

Finally Walking

Veronica Ponce, Miami Florida

Supplies: Image-editing software (Adobe Photoshop CS); fonts (1942 Report, 2P's Billboard, Gingersnap; Arial); brushes (truly-sarah.com and artist's own design)

Single-color photos

Tenika uses a series of colored photos in a single frame to create a cohesive look. Start with four photos and convert one to black-and-white. For the second one, open the channel mixer adjustment tool, choose the red output channel and increase the red value +100 leaving the other sliders untouched. Repeat for the third image, this time use the green output channel and the green slider, and for the fourth image do the same thing with the blue output channel and the blue slider. Create a page file with a yellow background, crop the photos to square and add them to the layout.

Frame the photos with a photo mat made using the round rectangle tool. Texturize the photo mat using the Noise > Texturize > Torn Edge filters. Use the line tool to make lines that create a flow through the layout, add clip-art elements and journaling to complete.

Baby How You've Grown
Tenika Morrison, Puyallup, Washington

Supplies: Image-editing software (Adobe Photoshop 7); fonts (Maszyna, Minion)

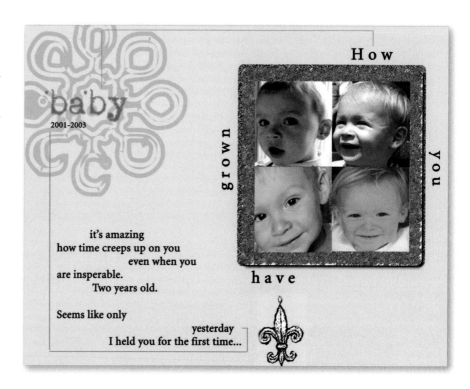

Seasonal colors

Rachel created this handsome page using fall colors to tint her photos. Start with a main photo and convert it to sepia. Crop the photo and duplicate it so you have one large and three cropped versions. Colorize the small images using the Hue/Saturation tool so that each is a different fall color. Create a background using colored shapes and textures of your choice and apply drop shadows to the layers to suggest stacked papers. Add the photos over the background. Rachel includes a word washer, twine and a library tag all of which she created herself. She also includes the date of the photo and finishes with a title created in clear text with the overlay blend mode applied to highlight the words.

Fall in Love
Rachel Dickson, Calgary, Alberta, Canada

Supplies: Image-editing software (Adobe Photoshop CS); fonts (Book Antiqua, Crack Babies)

Saturated-color blocks

The yellow and black from her son's T-shirt and the school bus directed Veronica's approach for this page. Use the Eyedropper tool to select your main color and then draw a rectangle next to the photo. Keep the emphasis on your main subject by lowering the opacity on any other large photo that could detract attention from it. For the smaller photos, have fun with color using Hue/Saturation to over-saturate the colors. If your subject is part of a group and you want to emphasize it, use the Rectangular Marquee tool to copy and paste it into a new layer on top and give it a different coloring than the main photo. Finally, separate your photo blocks with thick lines. In this case, the lines were actually created using the Rectangle tool. Finally, add your font and journaling, preferably over the lightened photo.

Summer Camp
Veronica Ponce, Miami, Florida

Supplies: Image-editing software (Adobe Photoshop CS); fonts (Goudy Old Style, Viper Nora)

Saturated-color photo collage

Stacy creates a colorful background using textures and gradients to blend her photos without obvious transitions or gaps. Start with a noise-sample gradient and adjust the color model until the gradient contains the right mix of colors for the project. Add texture with two photos (Stacy uses a close-up of some sand and a wall of ferns), de-saturate these and blur them and then adjust the blend mode and opacity for each layer until you have a nice background image. Add the four photos and apply blend modes to each to achieve a pleasing result—Stacy uses the linear light on two of her photos and hard light on the other two. Use custom-created maze brushes to decorate the edges and emphasize the theme of the layout. Finish with the title and journaling.

Maze
Stacy Fox-Myers, Fremont, California

Supplies: Image-editing software (Adobe Photoshop Elements 2); fonts (CK's Marker and Scratchy Box; Aquiline, Bustamalaka, Decker, Dominican, Kingsthings Printing Kit, Loosie Script, MA Sexy, Marcelle Script, Migraine Serif, Papyrus, Pharmacy, Problem Secretary, Saginaw, Stamp Act, Times and Times Again)

amandaloren

Brushes and filters

Veronica makes the large photo the focal point, and works the layout around it. Select a powerful main photo to enlarge; de-saturate if using a color photo. Use the levels or brightness/contrast feature to make image as "contrasty" as possible. If some areas of the photo are too light, use the burn tool to darken them. If any areas of the background remain, erase them completely. Use a Photoshop brush at 50 percent opacity to blend the edges of the photo to bleed into the background. Move photo to the upper right corner of the page. Use the rectangle tool to add a block of color along lower edge of page. In the layer menu, select Rasterize Shape. Use the filter Sketch/Halftone pattern to add horizontal lines to the rectangle in colors selected in the Foreground/Background. Add a smaller duplicate photo or a new image over rectangle at corner, reducing opacity so halftone pattern shows through. Use the brush or line tool to divide the top portion of your page from the bottom. Finish page by adding title and name and any embellishments (shapes, brushes, etc.), changing the opacity as desired to achieve the desired look.

Beautiful Amanda Loren
Veronica Ponce, Miami, Florida

Supplies: Image-editing software (Adobe Photoshop CS), font (Century Gothic), brush (personal design), flower clip art (source unknown)

Semitransparent layers

Helen uses a photo of a bright pink flower as a background for this page showing her young niece Molly. Size a photo suitable to use for a page background large enough to fill the page. Place a layer filled with white over the top and adjust its transparency downwards to make it semitransparent and mute the colors. Cut a flower from another image and paste it three times to use as a page accent adding a drop shadow to each. Cut the subject from another photo and paste into the page, sizing it to fill the page. Add a small white rectangle to the bottom corner, apply a paper texture to it and create a torn-edge look by erasing its edges. Apply chalk using a soft, low-opacity paintbrush. Create the title text and enhance it using a bevel and shadow effect.

Pretty in Pink
Helen Bradley, Santa Rosa, California

Supplies: Image-editing software (Jasc Paint Shop Pro 8); fonts (Baccus, Incised 901 BT)

pretty in PINK

Our little girl Molly - you look so pretty before your big evening out. It's so wonderful to see you growing up and into such a self possessed and fun young woman. I'm also so proud that you're equally comfortable at the beach surfing as dressed up for a big party

Warm-color filters

Yvette uses warm colors and filters to create a soft and sentimental look here. Start with a red textured background and drag the photos onto the canvas. Add a photo of a flower and alter it using Sketch > Conte Crayon to give it a drawn look. Set the photo layer blend mode to overlay or screen to blend the photos and soften them so the background shows through them. Use the Eraser on the edges of the photos and use geometric brushes to blend them. Add color to the page using the Variations dialog and choose a "more red" setting. Create dimensional text to finish the page.

Sweet Miracle

Yvette Ibarra-Keohuloa, Waipahu, Hawaii
Photos: Sherikia Jones, New York, New York

Supplies: Image-editing software (Adobe Photoshop); geometric brush (Magic Box); fonts (Aquiline); texture (ti-fi.com)

Varying opacities

Veronica first placed her photos on a white background and then superimposed blocks of color. If you're trying to achieve this look, be sure to keep at least one photo at 100 percent opacity so that your page doesn't look washed out. Extract the main photo from its background to give the subject more emphasis. If your original photos are too harsh, you can lighten them without lowering the opacity using the Saturation feature in Hue/Saturation. This can also be done for selected colors and not just the whole image. Select the color for the shapes from the main photo using the Eyedropper tool. Simple rectangles in different opacities add softness and consistency. After adding color, use Erase to erase parts of the photos that may overlap each other. This is a simple way of blending and, since the color blocks are over the image, it works just as well as applying a layer mode. By painting a final brush in a color overlay mode around the edges, you can soften and age the final page.

Pure

Veronica Ponce, Miami, Florida

Supplies: Image-editing software (Adobe Photoshop CS), fonts (Little Days, Primer Print)

Gaussian-blur aging

Celeste gives her old car a fine send-off with this attractive photo collage. Begin with a new image and create the papers for the background. Use the Add Noise filter set to 113 percent then the Pixelate Crystallize filter set at 180 and the Image, Adjust, Photo filter, Warming 80 at 80-percent strength. Finish with a Motion blur at 90 degrees and 999 strength. The result is a striped background. Use your choice of brushes to create a distressed and sanded look and layer over this text layers with the word "wheels" in various fonts. Repeat the process for the pale pink/red paper, this time apply the Pixelate Mosaic filter instead of Crystallize and for the blur use a Gaussian Blur at 25 percent. Create the brads using a custom shape tool and then AutoFX DreamSuite plug-in for the metallic surface. Create the ribbon in a similar way to the striped paper but omit the warming filter and use a texture pattern fill layer in its place. Add the large photo and apply a sepia tone to it and then a light Gaussian Blur before de-saturating it to age it. Create the edges using the Eraser with a fancy brush shape.

Our Car Duchess
Celeste Vardaman, Dallas, Texas

Supplies: Image-editing software (Adobe Photoshop CS); filter (Auto FX DreamSuite); brush (Seraphim); wheels brush (1greeneye.net); fonts (source unknown)

Gaussian-blur glow

Ronalyn makes this photo of her sons wearing their bowling shoes the focus of this snappy page celebrating a family bowling night. Apply a glow effect to your main photo by first selecting the focus of the image—here it is the shoes—using the Lasso tool. Brighten the selection but leave the original color intact. Invert the selection so everything but the focus of the image is selected and apply a Gaussian Blur and then de-saturate the area to remove the color. Copy the photo to the final layout, which is a series of similar themed photos on a black background. Add text and a title to finish.

Ready for Bowling
Ronalyn Barut, Honolulu, Hawaii

Supplies: Image-editing software (Adobe Photoshop 7); font (Monument)

Radial-blur blending

Janice blends her photo with a blurred version of the same photo for this touching layout. Start with the 12 x 12" size file and copy the photo into it. Duplicate this photo layer and size the duplicate to the full image size. Use a Radial Blur set to the Zoom option and an Amount of 85. Duplicate the photo again and crop closely to leave just the subjects. Duplicate the blurred layer and place it under this layer and blend the two layers and then merge them. Reduce the size of the merged layer and angle it on the image. On a new layer, add a stroke line to outline the photo and add a bevel to it for dimension. Finish with text angled to align with the photo.

Tender Moments

Janice Dye-Szucs, Oshawa, Ontario, Canada

Supplies: Image-editing software (Adobe Photoshop CS); fonts (Bernie, Typewriter)

Radial-blur movement

Rachel's layout features a photo of her son playing at the park. To heighten the impression of movement, duplicate the photo on a second layer and add a Radial Blur to the new duplicate layer. Use the Elliptical Marquee to select the area to remain in focus and soften the edges with a large feather. Invert the selection, set the colors to the default black-and-white and click the Layer-Mask icon—you'll see the focused part of the image through the surrounding blur. Create background papers using colors sampled from the image—here Rachel samples colors from the playground equipment to create blue, white and yellow striped papers and the gravel texture on the gray paper. Digitally tear the striped paper and layer it over the gray paper at the top and under the gray paper at the foot of the page. Add stitching to the top and bottom of the photo and create a stencil effect with a single character (here the letter C) using Glow and Shadow Layer Styles.

Courage

Rachel Dickson, Calgary, Alberta, Canada

Supplies: Image-editing software (Adobe Photoshop CS); fonts (Antique Type, Bookman Oldstyle, Impact)

Motion-blur title

By adding a Motion Blur to the title, Veronica conveys the physical activity taking place in these photos. Achieving this look requires only two steps. Duplicate your title in another layer. Use a motion blur in the bottom layer of your text and lower the opacity. For the photos, choose one large image that shows the activity and then place other smaller photos around it. Try to take pictures from different angles, or crop your photos in different ways to make the page flow with movement but try to keep the viewer's eye focused on the large photo. The smaller photos should help tell the story, but the large one is the main attraction. Add brushes, elements or shapes over the photos and don't be afraid to cover parts of the photos with these. Try to keep just one color photo (preferably the large one) and de-saturate the others. For coloring consistency, add a gradient map on the top level and experiment with different layer modes for different looks. In this case, the Gradient Layer is an Overlay but different modes give you different effects so play a little before committing to one.

Movement
Veronica Ponce, Miami, Florida

Supplies: Image-editing software (Adobe Photoshop CS), fonts (Hootie!, Felix Titling, Misproject), brushes

Leather and crackle filters

Leather and crackled paint provide a perfect backdrop for this attractive image. Sally creates the background texture using Alien Skin's Splat and Auto FX's DreamSuite to give a leatherlike grain with a crackle finish. Over this add an enlarged section of the main photo, and use the eraser tool to erase everything but the subject's eyes. Use the overlay layer blend mode to blend the eyes into the textured background. Create the ribbons using the page curl filter and then modify them further using the mesh warp tool so they look like ribbons. Sally creates her pearl bead accents using a picture tube she created herself but you can get a similar result by selecting and copying pearls from a photo of a pearl necklace. If you create a picture tube with pictures of pearls use the VectorTube script to create the frame for the journal block around the edges of the rectangular shape. Add your title and journaling in an appropriate font to complete the finish.

The Eyes Have It
Sally Beacham, East Waterboro, Maine

Supplies: Image-editing software (Auto FX DreamSuite, AV Bros Page Curl 2 plug-in, Jasc Paint Shop Pro 9); fonts (Edwardian Script, French Script, Garamond, pixelnook.home.comcast.net's VectorTube)

Brushes and layer masks

Blending photos into a background with brushes and layer masks helps Jeanette create a digital masterpiece. First, make background layer using brushes. Add photo in another layer and rotate it. Duplicate the background layer over the photo layer. Add a Layer Mask to this layer and draw with a soft black Brush to "erase" and allow your photo to show through. To give the photo a tinted and aged feel that more closely resembles a painting, add a Gradient Mask to recolor it and reduce the opacity. Add title to finish layout.

Hope is a Waking Dream
Jeanette Rubio, Miami, Florida

Supplies: Image-editing software (Adobe Photoshop CS); fonts (JSL Ancient, Scriptina)

Paint-filter opacity

Michelle creates a multilayer painted effect as her page background. Create the background starting with a single photo enlarged to fill the layout. Clone away any distracting or unwanted elements leaving the image uncluttered. Duplicate the layer a few times and apply different paint effects to each layer including the Paint Daubs and the Palette Knife effects. For each layer, apply the effect then reduce the opacity until you get the desired result. Use the Page Curl effect (Paint Shop Pro) to curl the photo edge and copy the photo into the page as a new layer. Use the shape tool to create lines to frame the piece and add word art effects using multiple fonts and the text tool.

The Path of Life
Michelle Shefveland, Sauk Rapids, Minnesota
Photos: Michael Bjork, St. Paul, Minnesota

Supplies: Image-editing software (Adobe Photoshop Elements 2.0, Jasc Paint Shop Pro 8); fonts (1942 Report, Bambino, Garamond, myfonts.com's P22 Cezanne)

CHAPTER

silly Cutie

mix a little
foolishness
with your prudence
it's good to be
silly
at the right moment.
Horace

sebastian

Having Fun With Fonts

You don't have to be a graphic artist to understand how to work with fonts successfully. In this chapter, you'll discover how simple it is to turn your page titles and journaling into stylish works of art. With the thousands of fonts available on CD or from the Internet, you'll find a few basic rules of typography helpful to know before you start designing a computer scrapbook page.

There are generally two types of fonts—serif (has little lines or curves resembling pen strokes called serifs at the ends of each character) and sans serif (doesn't have these embellishments). Serif fonts help the eye move from word to word and are generally easier to read than sans serif fonts. With all the fun and fancy lettering available, classic fonts might seem a little boring, but they go with anything and are easy to read.

Choosing appropriate fonts for page titles is more critical than the journaling fonts because of the titles' importance. First, consider the look that you want to convey—whether whimsical, serious, funny, sophisticated, cute, classic or elegant. The title font should contrast with the journaling font in terms of style, size, color or boldness. In other words, don't mix similar fonts.

With fonts, less is more. Too many fonts compete for attention and clutter the layout. Unless a variety of fonts is a deliberate part of page design, use no more than three to four fonts at a time. Avoid using all capitalized, boldfaced and/or underlined words, as they tend to distract and slow down reading. To emphasize a word or phrase, simply use the italic font.

Font size is also an important consideration for both title and journaling fonts. Obviously, large point sizes are more appropriate for page titles, while a point size of 12 to 20 works well for journaling. Experiment with different sizes to find the one that best fits the layout, and practice keeping title size in proportion to the size of journaling and other page elements.

Once you've experimented with different looks, start to experiment with dressing up fonts and adding unique finishes to them. Remember, the main goal with fonts is readability and a polished appearance. Have fun!

Storytelling with script

Heartfelt journaling in a white script font helps Helen tell the story of sharing her pregnancy with her husband. Using image-editing software that supports layers, convert the photo to black-and-white and use the history brush to paint back the color in the bow. Another option is to duplicate the original photo layer so you have two identical photos on top of each other. Select the top photo in the layer palette and convert it to black-and-white; then erase the portions of the black-and-white photo layer where you want the original color to show through, as Helen did for the bow. To do this, select the eraser tool with an appropriately sized and shaped brush. As you get closer to the edges, decrease the size of your brush. Finish with the white journaling and black title in front of image in chosen colors.

Christmas Gift

Helen Shi-Yuen, Lawrenceville, New Jersey

Supplies: Image-editing software (Adobe Photoshop); fonts (dafont.com's Old Script; Scriptina)

Ahh..the good 'ol furrowed brow from the Cruz-Segarra side. Passed down from generation to generation. Papi to Mama to Ashton.

Mixing script and serif fonts

Bold blocks of color make the title and journaling treatments leap from Tenika's page. Use the Custom Shape tool to draw different rectangle and square shapes with black, yellow and red foreground colors. Then crop the photo and size it to intersect the blocks; add drop shadows with the layer style palette. Create bold initials in opposing colors with the Text tool and set on the square blocks. Set off the 'f' with an imperfect circular custom shape drawn in black. Use the Line tool to add four opposing short lines, bringing focus to the title. Add a drop shadow to the single word title and a text block of journaling to complete the page.

Frown

Tenika Morrison, Puyallup, Washington

Supplies: Image-editing software (Adobe Photoshop 7.0); fonts (myfonts.com's High Tower Text, Palatino Linotype; scrapvillage.com's Pegsanna HMK)

My Sons

Sticky fingers, dirty face
Rugs and pillows out of place
Cars and tractors here and there
Blocks and boats are everywhere
Gold and silver have I none,
But worth a million are my sons.

2004

August

Ryan Adam Kyle

Skewed fonts

Skewed text, with deep shadows, creates a strong visual element on Tracy's page. Start with a canvas texture for the background. Then paste the photo on the background, moving to desired position and resize. Add date tag accent included in the software. Use a text color that matches a color in the photo, in this case the deep red of the tractor. Add title using a large point size; skew it choosing Transform > Distort and also add the drop shadow. Repeat for the poem, skewing in the same manner. For the month and names, rotate the text vertically, adding a drop shadow to the names.

My Sons
Tracy Johnson, Memory Makers magazine

Supplies: Image-editing software (Ulead PhotoExpress); font (Mom's Typewriter)

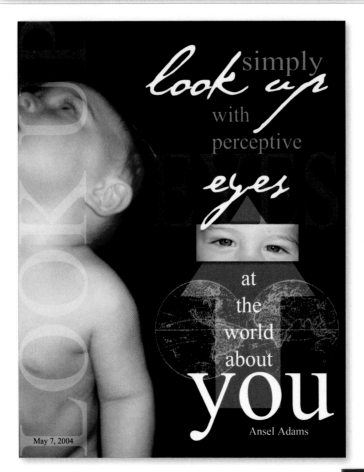

Rotated fonts

Ronnie's use of fonts creates a monochromatic, graphic-styled layout backed by black and set off with intricate white font work. Staggering script fonts with serif fonts in different sizes makes an attractive combination, and adjusting the opacity for a translucent look adds to the appeal. Use image-editing software to create separate text boxes for each word, allowing customization and exact positioning as separate layers. For the title, rotate the text 90 degrees counterclockwise, running parallel with the image, which was extracted from the background of the original photograph. Add an arrow in gray using a custom shape in the software, as well as clip art to create more depth and dimension. Finish the piece by adding a cropped close-up image set off with a drop shadow.

Look Up
Ronnie McCray, St. James, Missouri

Supplies: Image-editing software (Adobe Photoshop Elements 2.0); fonts (Hannibal Lector, myfonts.com's P22 Cezanne; Times New Roman); world clip art (source unknown)

Large font background

Grunge textures and bold font treatments complement the carnival theme on Ronnie's page. Start with a deep red fill layer and add a messy black edge by "painting" with various standard brushes. Convert a Ferris wheel photograph into a custom brush to "stamp" in black on the background. Use the image-editing software's Custom Shapes and Layer Style to simulate red glass photo corners, letter pebbles and a round brad. Merge a rectangular shape and two different circular shapes into one layer to create a tag. Stamp the Ferris wheel custom brush again on the tag, decreasing the brush size and selecting a pale gray foreground color. Add white and black text with a very faint layer of the word "Carnival" at the bottom of the page, adjusting opacity to 10 percent in the layer palette to make the text barely visible. Give the photo and tag a slight drop shadow in Layer Style for added depth.

Garish Carnival
Ronnie McCray, St. James, Missouri

Supplies: Image-editing software (Adobe Photoshop Elements 2.0); fonts (Hannibal Lector; myfonts.com's P22 Cezanne; Times New Roman); paper and elements (artist's own designs); Soomer layer style (Adobe.com)

Mix fonts tastefully

Cleverly done, font work can be a work of art in and of itself. Dena uses various type styles in different hues, sizes and orientations to effectively set off the candid shots of her son. When overlapping fonts, use contrast in the colors or opacity, so they can be easily read. Add each different font style as a separate layer with the text tool in order to have more control in positioning the text. Create the background with rectangular blocks of color; add a canvas texture to the red and custom brushwork throughout for a collage effect. Add grunge edges to the photos with brushes and the Eraser tool.

A Smile Can Happen
Dena Simoneaux, Henderson, Nevada

Supplies: Image-editing software (Adobe Photoshop CS); fonts (Dutch 801, Marcelle Script, McCarey, Roughwork, Scriptina); custom brushes (annikavonholdt.com; 1greeneye.net)

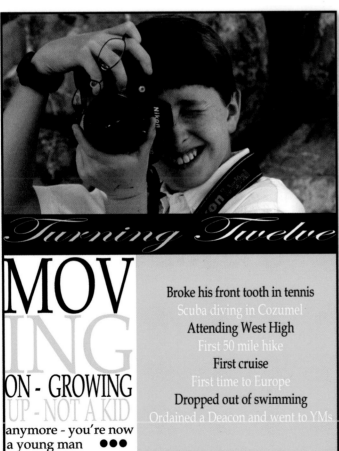

Alternated font colors

Switching off between black, white and yellow text and rectangular blocks makes Sande's classic page a showcase for her son's milestones to manhood. Wrapping the word "Moving" adds drama and aids in the block text formation, as does the decreasing font size and switching case as it moves downward. Add interest with bullet-style journaling by centering and alternating between black and white on a yellow block. The high-contrast black-and-white horizontal photo completes the graphic look. Add a thin black border for a final framing touch.

Turning Twelve
Sande Krieger, Salt Lake City, Utah

Supplies: Image-editing software (Adobe Photoshop 7); fonts (Bold Antiqua, Edwardian Script)

Beveled fonts

A large, beveled number balances the layout's photo by anchoring a large amount of neutral space on Ronnie's page and complements the linear flow of the photo. Select a trendy script font with an easy-to-read serif font for a crisp, clean look. Enhance a bold, black numeral with a sharp bevel from Layer Style in the image-editing software to make the number pop from the page. Add red and taupe rectangles as borders for the layout with the Custom Shape tool for further definition and to pull out the main colors in the photo.

High 5 Line-Up
Ronnie McCray, St. James, Missouri

Supplies: Image-editing software (Adobe Photoshop Elements 2.0); fonts (Hannibal Lector, myfonts.com's P22 Cezanne; Times New Roman)

Skewed fonts

Helen creates a whimsical page of her cute-as-a-bug Valentine using image-editing software's custom shapes, warped text and a frame plug-in. Form a base coat of yellow for the background for a bright photo; apply a jagged edge on the background and a stippled heart with Extensis PhotoFrame. Add impact to the title by skewing it with the Warp Text function. With this one-step feature, the amount and direction of the skew can be adjusted; Flag or Fish Eye are additional Warp Text options. Create the initial cap, in this case a variegated V, with a script font letter, then Rasterize, select the Magic Wand tool and fill with a linear gradient made up of a red foreground color and white background color.

Valentine
Helen Shi-Yuen, Lawrenceville, New Jersey

Supplies: Image-editing software (Adobe Photoshop); photo frame and edge (Extensis PhotoFrame); font (dafont.com's Chopin Script)

Bleeding fonts off page

Penny creates this vibrant layout for her daughter by layering words in different fonts and letting the text "bleed" right off the page. Use color cues from a flower photo to create a solid purple background and complementary green border. Frame focal photo by adding a rectangular preset shape beneath the photo layer to act as a mat, adding depth with a drop shadow. Anchor the photo with four yellow brads created with the circle preset shape and rounded-edge bevel. Add vibrant yellow font work as another decorative component for the background, with each line a different vector text layer for easier positioning. For the title, use the same three colors as in the layout—plus black—layering script fonts atop serif fonts, dark on top of light and small on top of big. Use a filter plug-in to give one word of the title a glowing effect.

Life that Enlightens the Soul
Penny Dutcher, Denver, Colorado

Supplies: Image-editing software (Corel Paint Shop Pro 7 and 8); fonts (1942 Report, American Classic Extra Bold, Anglia Script Standard, Arial, AS Snapper, Script Broadway BT); prose (twopeasinabucket.com); glow filter (Alien Skin Eye Candy 4000)

Repeated fonts

Use of repetitive words in the same fonts and subtle journaling help Susan bring consistency throughout a scrapbook album that documents her son's first year. Highlight each month's changes with a special page, using text as a design accent on color-blocked pages. Add rectangular blocks of color, texturized with faux finish brushes as well descriptive text, square beveled brads and a triad of photos placed on the background. De-saturate the color of two of photos and add a bevel effect. For the third photo, use Layer Blend Mode to add transparency and color harmony with the background. Repeat age word, in this case "Four," to make the page theme obvious and to add a contrasting border around the page. Blend the journaling into the background by reducing the opacity slightly.

Four Months
Susan Ratsey, Nesconset, New York

Supplies: Image-editing software (Adobe Photoshop CS); fonts (Franklin Gothic Demi Condensed Seraphim, Times and Times Again; Kingthings Printingkit; dafont.com's Easy Street)

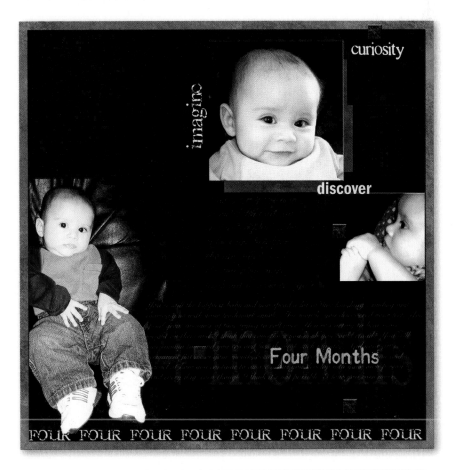

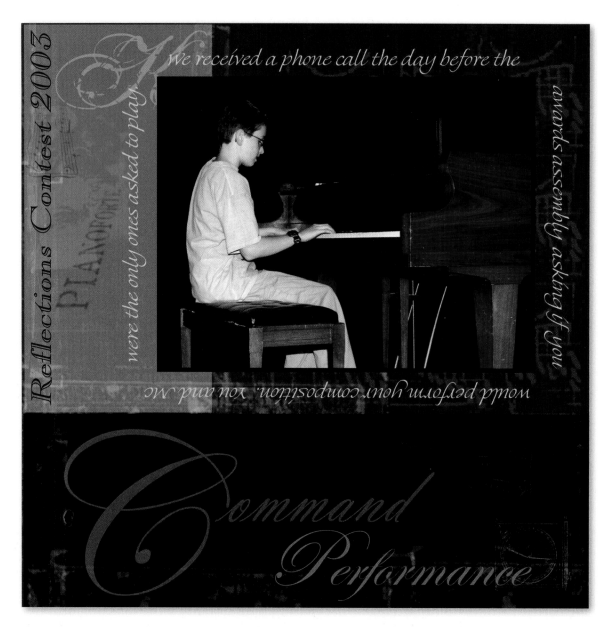

Fonts flowed in a frame

Framing the focal photo with text is easily done on Sande's page with four different text boxes/layers, each rotated to be parallel to the photo edge. Showcasing her son's musical abilities with the rich tones in the photo and classic fonts adds to timeless and masculine look of the page. Use custom brushes to stamp images on a color-blocked background, creating one-of-a-kind patterned paper, which can be re-used indefinitely. One unique feature of digital paper is the ability to change the colors to match different layouts and photos. Most image editors have color adjustment functions that are simple to execute.

Command Performance
Sande Krieger, Salt Lake City, Utah

Supplies: Image-editing software (Adobe Photoshop 7); fonts (Caslon Open Face, Edwardian Script, Fine Hand, Vladimir Script); custom brushes (studio.adobe.com)

Fonts on a curve

Flowing text on a curve or in a circle accentuates the photo theme on Ronnie's layout for great visual appeal. Create checkered background with a repeated Pattern Fill and Stamp solid sage mat with a globe brush. Make faux ribbon with the Rectangular Shape tool in yellow and a black punch label strip, both of which were erased to appear as if being threaded through slots in the circle-cropped photo. Following the shape of the park tunnel slide, add text on a circular path using the software's text tools. Another option to achieve a similar effect with Adobe Photoshop Elements, as Ronnie did, is to warp the text in two opposite arcs. For the title, rotate text 90 degrees clockwise, running parallel with the edge of the focal photo; adjust opacity of some text layers to make them appear translucent. Add fun Warp Text effects to individual words or sentences for interest and drop shadows to enhance the illusion of depth.

Healthful Play
Ronnie McCray, St. James, Missouri

Supplies: Image-editing software (Adobe Photoshop Elements 2.0); fonts (acme.com's Dymo Punch Label; Hank BT, Hannibal Lector; myfonts.com's P22 Cezanne; Times New Roman); globe brush (de.geocities.com)

Fonts used to crop photos

Unique text effects add movement to Andrea's page about her and her husband's 10th anniversary trip along Route 66. Start with a solid olive background that is used as a gauge to colorize the photo for a monochromatic look. To create the illusion that the photo was cut by the curve of the cursive font, enter the title using the text tool, rotate it 90 degrees clockwise and merge it with the photo. Use the Magic Wand selection tool set on contiguous to select everything to the right of the black text then cut this selected area from the merged layer. The remaining portion of the title, 66, is a cutout from a scan of a paper bag with the color removed. To duplicate this technique, add text, select it and then copy and paste this selection from the paper bag layer. Accentuate the number with a narrow black outline. Duplicate and enlarge this layer in different sizes, reducing the opacity for a subtle background pattern. Extract and repeat the road sign from the photo using the Selection tool and then paste as page accents.

Route 66
Andrea Sampson, Lathrop, Missouri

Supplies: Image-editing software (Adobe Photoshop CS); fonts (Century Schoolbook; CK's Cursive)

Custom printing with fonts

Not having a photo of her son with his birthday cake didn't stop Marsha from making a birthday page. Use image-editing software to extract cake from a different photo and paste it into second photo. Add child's name and age to the balloon bouquet in the photo, picking up a darker shade of the balloons with the Color Picker tool and rotating the text to look realistic. Use a simple white rectangle for a title mat and a black outline to finish the page.

The Big 7
Marsha Musselman, Lake City, Michigan

Supplies: Image-editing software (Microsoft Digital Image Pro 7); fonts (Calvin & Hobbs; Chatterbox's Fingerpaint, Jesse James)

Transparent fonts

Holly sneaks a translucent font treatment onto a feminine page about her daughter's talent for sneaking food. Start with a pale pink background. Create the darker pink flowers using a standard custom flower shape and positioning them where desired. After pasting in the photo, create a photo mat with the Rectangular Shape tool just slightly larger than the photo and position beneath the photo. Create the photo-filled word by typing the text, rasterizing it, selecting it with the Magic Wand tool and then copying and pasting the selected area from the photo layer. Add a 130-degree drop shadow to make the title stand out. Add prominence to the initial cap, in this case an A, with a large point size; rasterize and then texturize it with the Noise filter set at a uniform, monochromatic 30-percent setting.

Audrey Food Sneak
Holly VanDyne, Mansfield, Ohio

Supplies: Image-editing software (Adobe Photoshop CS); font (Verdana)

Photo-filled fonts

Doris cleverly uses fonts and a photo to create part of her page title. To create this type of collage, loosely draw a large feathered selection around the focal photo, select the inverse and delete the background. Repeat this with a photo of a cornstalk, positioning it over the main photo to create a sense of depth. Make a thin frame around the edges by drawing lines to resemble overlapping boxes using a brush with a fade so that it is thicker in the start than the finish. Then select a portion of the frame, feather the selection and apply a Wave filter. Blend photo in the lower right corner into page by setting the opacity of the layer to 16 percent. Create the photo-filled title by typing the text over a portion of a photo, rasterize it, select it with the Magic Wand tool and then copy and paste the selected area from the photo layer. To make the green underlay, enlarge this same selection about 10 pixels and fill with a green to match the cornstalks (on a new layer). Apply a drop shadow to both text layers to give title more prominence. Use an Overlay Blend mode on the script portion of title for richness and transparency.

Little Seedlings
Doris Castle, Fonda, New York

Supplies: Image-editing software (Adobe Photoshop); fonts (1001fonts.com's Baby Kruffy; fonts.com's Carpenter ICG); poem (twopeasinabucket.com)

You look at me and see
a child so small and young.
My growing season has barely begun.
There are things you don't see,
Hidden deep inside of me,
Special gifts I came with
the day of my birth.
Little seeds of greatness
that I brought to earth.

Little seeds will grow and grow,
Little leaves begin to show.
And just like those seeds,
I'm full of possibilities.
Even the tallest trees,
started as little seeds.

Oh that sweet baby face...

Your first year has gone by so fast! I wish you could stay my little baby forever.
You are the joy in my life and the light in my eye.

~ Love, Mommy

Photo collage font monogram

What fun to use an initial monogram as the basis for a collage of photos as Stephanie did. Create the green and plum background with the Rectangular Shape tool and the Render Clouds filter. To the white rectangle add yellow circles by "stamping" with a large hard edge round brush. Create a large rectangular-shaped photomontage by layering different photos, adjusting the Opacity and Layer Blend modes until you like the end result. Use a chunky font and the Text tool to type the three initials over the collage and rasterize the text. With the Magic Wand tool, select the three letters, then copy and paste this selection from the photos. Delete the original text and the original collage of photos (or make them invisible so you can edit again, if needed). Add a drop shadow to the initials and white journaling to finish the art.

AMK
Stephanie Kean, Aurora, Colorado

Supplies: Image-editing software (Adobe Photoshop 7); fonts (Arial, Arial Black; fonts.com's Monotype Corsiva)

Rotated fonts as background

Playful text rotation adds to the childlike playfulness of Diane's special heritage photos of herself and her brothers. Use the Color Picker tool to select color from photos to use for background color. Create the flowing ribbon effect using a plug-in filter. Repeat 3s in text and numerals and add to the background using the Text tool, each on their own layer in varying transparencies; rotate and move around the page using the Deform tool. Use a standard layer mask to create the jagged edges on three small accent photos and set off with light-colored mats extending a tad beyond photo edges. Add journaling to the bottom of the page using the hue of the blue sky in the photo.

Three Amigos
Diane Petersmarck, Evanston, Illinois
Photos: Jerry Wiessner, Lodi, Wisconsin

Supplies: Image-editing software (Corel Paint Shop Pro 8); fonts (myfonts.com's Park Ave D; pccrafter.com's PCMunchkin, PCSpeckle; scrapvillage.com's Pegsanna HMK, Scriptina; Succotash HMK [source unknown]); Dragonfly Sinedot filter (philipp-spoeth.de)

Font collage word art

Dena shares a block-styled collage of photos of her son at the beach intermingled with layers of word art in subtle coastal hues. Select photos for the collage, drag them on the white background, size them, arrange with the Move tool and then cut off any extra with the Rectangular Marquee tool and Edit > Cut. Make sage green, buttercream and blue rectangular blocks with the Custom Shape tool; position over the smaller accent photos and border blocks, decreasing the opacity of those over the photos. Add texture to blue blocks with custom brushes. Create word art by using the Text tool and the Color Picker tool (picking up colors from the blocks) and a collection of grunge-style fonts in script and serif, each on their own layer and in varying opacities. Scatter, layer and vary the words and journaling. Rotate the title along the page edge. Finish with a crisscross grid of white lines created with thin, intersecting, rectangular shapes.

Amelia Island
Dena Simoneaux, Henderson, Nevada

Supplies: Image-editing software (Adobe Photoshop CS); fonts (CK's Maternal; dafont.com's Adorable, Marcelle Script, Stamp Act; McCarey; myfonts.com's Carpenter; Dutch 801); custom brushes (1greeneye.net)

Fonts as background or with shadows

Andrea constructs a retro page using an Internet compilation of 1980s happenings as a background. Create the grungy striped background using different colors with the Line tool. Apply a pattern made from a crumpled grocery bag; set the Blend mode to Multiply to bring out the color of the stripes but keep the crumpled texture. Make vellum using a white square custom shape; lower its opacity to 50 percent for transparency. The smiley face clips start as a rounded rectangle shape, then space is cut out of them for the clip portion. Draw a smiley face on separate layers with various tools, then bevel and emboss and apply a gradient for a stamped, plastic look. To make one appear as if clipped on the vellum, position it beneath the vellum in the layer palette, duplicate it and then erase the clip part from the duplicate. Repeat this for all three clips. Make white rectangles for paper strips. Make a circle shape; add same effects as clips for brads. Follow similar steps to make a paper clip: Use a custom paper clip shape and erase a portion of it. Give one photo a torn edge by "ripping" it with the Lasso tool and fill a layer with the photo shape with white; nudge it out a bit from behind the photo, followed with a pattern for texture. Use Layer Style to add soft drop shadows to the photos and elements. Complete the page three layers of the titles using the Text tool; stagger placement and vary opacity for depth.

Children of the 80s
Andrea Sampson, Lathrop, Missouri
Photos: Beth Sampson, Pocatello, Idaho

Supplies: Image-editing software (Adobe Photoshop CS); font (Century Schoolbook)

Clip art in fonts

Penny's computer layout shows the fun possibilities of using clip art over fonts to create unique titles. Create a patterned, textured and layered background using filters, brushes and varying opacities. Add photos over black rectangles. Create digital page accents as explained throughout Chapter 4. Select a wide font and fill inner portions with a theme font for the first part of title, deleting the selected animal silhouette to create the cut out. Choose a simple font for the remainder of title.

Zootiful
Penny Dutcher, Denver, Colorado

Supplies: Image-editing software (20/20, Jasc Paint Shop Pro 7); fonts (flyerstarter.com's SF Gothican Condensed); postcard (The Denver Zoo); corrugated cardboard texture (Redfield's Jama Filter); torn-edge effect (Alien Skin Eye Candy 4000)

Fonts used in a game

Doris compares life to a childhood game in this whimsical layout. Patterned text was created using the Candy Cane typeface, which was rasterized in order to modify the colors. She selected the white portions with the Magic Wand tool, filled with a light pink, selected the black portions and filled with a darker pink. Bevel and Outer Glow Layer Styles were applied for dimension. The background was created by filling with a radial rainbow gradient and a texture Layer Style. Using the real game as a reference, Doris created a winding game board with skewed adjoining rectangular shapes, each in a different pastel hue. Images from the Internet were scattered on white rectangles for game cards, and the photos were cut and pasted on the page with loosely feathered selections.

Castle Land
Doris Castle, Fonda, New York

Supplies: Image-editing software (Adobe Photoshop CS); fonts (Arial; fontmenu.com's Candy Cane; Lucida Handwriting); card images (Hasbro.com)

Fonts used for magazine cover

Margie creates this witty and fun magazine cover-styled page showcasing her encounters with parenting. Start with a candid portrait re-sized to 8½ x 11". Use the Text tool to add the white text blocks on each side of the page. Give the title a small Bevel Layer Style for more definition. To make the title appear beneath photo subject, use the Freehand Selection tool to Copy/Paste his head on a new layer above the text. Use the Healing Brush to help clean up the background wall and draw the Selection tool around the eggs while adjusting the Hue to a deeper color in photo where desired. To create the bar code, add a white rectangle and black vertical lines with the Custom Shape tool. For the barcode number, type the date with the Text tool.

Parenting
Margie Lundy, Greenfield, Ohio

Supplies: Image-editing software (Adobe Photoshop); font (Arial)

Stenciled fonts

Metal and embossed letters add sheen and dimension to Angela's energetic page of her sons' adventures. Using a Pen Ink filter in Digital Image Pro, Angela created the textured red background then brought it into Adobe Photoshop to add more depth with the burn tool. For the red fontwork, she used Bevel, Emboss and Drop Shadow Layer Styles. To make the realistic E stencil, Angela copied the textured background paper, de-saturated and darkened it, then cut the Stencil font out of it using the Selection tool. Metal letters were created using a Zebra Chrome filter from Eye Candy, plus an inner bevel and drop shadow. The strips of fabric were made by copying, pasting, de-saturating and darkening a thin rectangular selection from the background paper. White text was added on top of the fabric strip for a twill tape look. To create the ski rope extending out of the picture into an eyelet, she selected the rope using the Magic Wand tool, copied, pasted, re-positioned and completed with a drop shadow.

Red Energy
Angela Svoboda, Ord, Nebraska

Supplies: Image-editing software (Adobe Photoshop CS, Microsoft Digital Image Pro Suite 9); fonts (dafont.com's 4990810; larabie-fonts.com's Euphorigenic; scrapvillage.com's Blackjack; unionfonts.com's Stencil); white frame Photoshop action (epaper-press.com); Zebra Chrome filter (Alien Skin EyeCandy 3.1)

Stamped and label-maker fonts

With Paint Shop Pro, Grace made a spirited page of her kids' fun in the sun. Starting with a white raster background at 8½ x 11", Grace used the browse function to find her photo and drag it onto the layout. She duplicated this photo layer, reduced one in size applied a Dreamy Photo filter to soften and act as a journaling mat. Using the original untouched photo as a color guide, she made a large rectangle with the Marquee Selection tool and filled it with black (on a new layer below the focal photo), then drew lines of different coordinating colors and varied thickness with the Line tool within this selection. For the mat, she drew a white rectangle shape slightly larger than the photo and added a drop shadow. On the top and bottom of the striped background she added black text with the Punch Label typeface, and then drew narrow white vertical lines making the label tape look cut in sections. On the original white background still exposed, she drew custom circles and circular rings with different coordinating colors, giving a retro polka-dot look. The green strips were rectangular shapes in which a weave pattern was applied. The stitching is simply dashed lines drawn with the Line tool, to which a slight drop shadow is applied. Fonts create the faux rubber stamped "Ball" and button words automatically. The rectangular blocks of color beneath them were airbrushed along the edges for a chalked effect. Journaling was added in white above the blurred photo and accented with a drop shadow.

Having a Ball
Grace Castillo, Anaheim, California

Supplies: Image-editing software (Corel Paint Shop Pro); fonts (2P's Gift; scrapvillage.com's Black Boys on Mopeds, Cupcake, Hootie, Punch Label); Dreamy Photo filter plug-in (Auto FX Dream Suite)

Fonts sampler

Ake created this fun digital alphabet to inspire you to play with fonts, effects and filters for one-of-a-kind letters and numbers. Bevel, emboss, gradient, outer glow and drop shadow Layer Styles are common functions used to add dimension and sheen. Brushwork adds depth to edges and Filters add texture or metallic sheens.

Alphabet Grid

Ake Harini Pangestuti, Chicago, Illinois

Supplies: Image-editing software (Adobe Photoshop CS); filter plug-ins (Alien Skin Eye Candy 4000, Xenofex; Auto FX DreamSuite); fonts (sourced beneath each letter)

Brock Script (dafont.com)

Round shape > color edges with brush > add top round shape > color with brush > bevel, emboss both layers

Acklin (webpagepublicity.com)

Round shape > Alien Skin Eye Candy 4000 filter > distort > wave > chrome > outdoor

Beautiful ES (fontfreak.com)

Alien Skin Xenofex 2 > bow, flag; Brad: layer style > bevel, emboss; Red chalk: brushes > chalk

Balzac (dafont.com)

Edges: filter > distort > wave; Clip: layer style > bevel, emboss; Letter D: layer style > bevel, emboss

Ambrosia (acidfonts.com)

Letter and background: layer style > bevel, emboss

Three keys form letter F

Alien Skin Eye Candy 4000 > Silver accent: adjust layer style (gradient and satin setting)

Allegro (dafont.com)

Envelope: layer style > shadow; Letter G: Layer style > bevel, emboss

Times New Roman

Layer atop two round, colored shapes

Zeppelin (highfonts.com)

Alien Skin Eye Candy 4000 > chrome > shiny penny

Zapfino Linotype (myfonts.com)

Alien Skin Eye Candy 4000 > white background > layer style > outer glow

Typist Bold (webpagepublicity.com)

Keyboard key: layer style > bevel, emboss > contour

Shishoni Brush CAC (fontseek.com)

Alien Skin Xenofex 2 > ribbon, flag; Eyelet: Alien Skin Eye Candy 4000 > chrome > outdoor; Border: edit > stroke

Acid Romantics (acidfonts.com)

Mesh: layer style > bevel, emboss; Letter M: layer style > bevel, emboss

Times New Roman

Typewriter key: layer style > bevel, emboss; Gold rim: layer style > gradient

Broadview (grsites.com)

Alien Skin Xenofex 2 > torn paper > rip open; Frame: Alien Skin Eye Candy 4000 > bevel, emboss

Preciosa (grsites.com)

Alien Skin Eye Candy 4000 > Album: edit > transform > distort; Eyelet: Alien Skin Eye Candy 4000 > chrome > outdoor; Fiber: brushes > fuss ball, grass

Pharmacy (grsites.com)

Alien Skin Xenofex 2 > ribbon, flag; Metal: Alien Skin Eye Candy 4000 > chrome > outdoor; Stitching: white lines; Edges/rounded wrap or frame: layer style > bevel, emboss

Old Constructed Caps (dafont.com)

Folder: two rectangle shapes, with rounded corners, overlapped

Old Script (dafont.com)

Wavy paper shape; Metal: Alien Skin Eye Candy 4000 > chrome > yard

Occidental (highfonts.com)

Button: layer style > bevel, emboss satin; Letter T: edit > transform > distort

Acklin (webpagepublicity.com)

Handmade stitches brush; Outline letter U; Texture: filter > texture > texturizer > burlap

Minion (highfonts.com)

Alien Skin Eye Candy 4000 > cork board > filter > noise > add noise, then filter > pixelate > crystallize; Staples: Alien Skin Eye Candy 4000 > chrome > outdoor; Letter V: layer style > shadow

Black Chancery (webfxmall.com)

Alien Skin Eye Candy 4000 > buckle > chrome > outdoor

Marriage Script (dafont.com)

Fiber: brushes > fuzzy ball; Button: layer style > bevel, emboss

Alien Skin Xenofex 2 > zipper; Metal: > adjust gradient setting > layer style > gradient; Fabric > Alien Skin Xenofex 2 > flag

Plastique (dafont.com)

Slide: layer style > bevel, emboss

The heroic spirit will not fail to dream of rugged paths. Henry David Thoreau

happy go lucky rugged boy happy go lucky rugged boy happy go lucky rugged boy happy go lucky rugged boy

MARAMEC

RUGGED young man

Isaac is your typical 5 year old boy - he really loves to play outside in the mud and dirt. But he also loves to come inside to take a bath to soak in the water and play in the soap suds! He is a very happy young man!

Isaac

Creating Digital Page Accents

Similar to traditional scrapbooking, page accents or embellishments are the last touch of depth and texture you'll add to a computer-generated scrapbook page. Similarly as well, page accents should be used sparingly so as not to clutter the text and photo art you've already created on the background page. And the best news of all is that you can create with your computer all of the page accents you've grown to know and love from the world of traditional paper scrapbooking.

Design inspiration for page accents can come from anywhere, including art from traditional scrapbooking, the home and everything around you. Use a scanner to scan household objects and apply tools and filters to them to bring them to life, play with copyright-free clip art to mimic the look of rubber stamping and stickers or download ready-made digital accents and embellishments from the Web sites such as those mentioned on page 19.

Digital page accents are anything but flat. By applying artistic filters, plug-in effects or tool adjustments, two-dimensional page accents leap from your computer-generated scrapbook page with character, depth, sheen and texture.

By experimenting and playing with geometric shapes, layering and filters and plug-in effects, you'll be designing all of the beads and baubles, metallic, organic and textile accents your heart desires. From buttons to bottle caps and wooden slide mounts to fibers, anything is possible when a will to create the perfect digital page accent is just mouse clicks away.

Kaitlyn will be leaving for the mission field with her parents. They will be leaving for Roanoke, VA first. Then, they will go to Costa Rica for a year before they get to their final destination, Uruguay. Seth has grown up with Kaitlyn. They were in Kindergarten together! Aaron says that Kaitlyn is his girlfriend. We asked that Kaitlyn pose in a picture with Aaron, then Jacob had to get in the picture too! We will miss Pastor Paul, Pam, and Kaitlyn!

We'll miss **KAITLYN**

Buttons

Graphic lines, white space and buttons add interest to Talina's layout. Start with a white fill background; add square shapes of blue, cutting the inner portion to leave a thin square frame. Repeat this for a larger brown shape and duplicate both, repositioning where desired. Use these same two colors to create a nested trio of square photo mats, adding drop shadows and aging with different colored brushes and an Inner Glow Layer Style. Create three small brown square shapes and a long, brown rectangular shape; enhance with a Canvas Texture filter. Make blue ribbon the same way with an additional Motion Blur filter applied for a vertical ribbed look. Use blue round shapes to create buttons then add depth with Bevel, Contour and Drop Shadow Layer Styles. Cut the four holes with a circular Eraser brush; use the Line tool to make the X button stitch. Use Super Blade Pro to apply a metal effect to the ribbon charm. Add journaling in the white space and a cream title to layer above the brown border strip. Age the title with an eraser brush.

We'll Miss Kaitlyn
Talina Watterson, Kingsport, Tennessee

Supplies: Image-editing software (Adobe Photoshop CS); fonts (dafont.com's Crack Babies; simplythebest.net's Teletype); filter (Flaming Pear Super Blade Pro)

Buttons and appliqué

Ronnie's two-page layout showcases a photo of her dreaming family, accented with digital buttons and a cheery cherry appliqué. The two pages are created as one image; when ready to print, they are flattened then cut into two separate pages. Begin the cherry patterned paper by creating a green custom shape. Color the cherries red then duplicate and rotate the shape all over a gray-filled rectangle shape. Enlarge one of the cherry images and add a Burlap Texture filter and bevel for the appliqué. Apply patterns to mustard-, burgundy- and olive colored rectangles to create canvas papers. Add vellum text ribbons for page borders. Drag photo onto layout, then copy and crop squares of the faces; paste as accent photos. To create the rickrack, use the Custom Wave shape (comes in a set of three waves), cut out the extra two waves, compress it to make the waves closer and sharper; duplicate, connect end-to-end, merge and texturize. Make the tag and journal strips from rectangular shapes. For buttons, use two basic shapes—a circle and a cutout circle; stack in a group of four and thread with faux stitching and add different Plastic Layer Styles for color. Create thin rectangles for staples; apply the Chrome Layer Style. Create chunky tag eyelet with a circle shape, metal Layer Style and a round Eraser brush to cut the hole. Add a slight Drop Shadow Layer Style to all elements, papers and photos. Design the word art in different font styles, colors and orientations as described throughout the "Having Fun With Fonts" chapter.

Gaping Dreamers
Ronnie McCray, St. James, Missouri

Supplies: Image-editing software (Adobe Photoshop Elements 2.0); fonts (Hannibal Lector; myfonts.com's P22 Cezanne; Times New Roman)

Beads

Small, textured baubles add pop to Angela's digital page. First, enlarge the black-and-white photo to fill most of the page, hand-tint with brushes and add a Canvas texture to a white rectangle made with the Shape tool. Create the sandals with a hand-drawn shape then apply a Texture effect and a bead with Picture Tube. Duplicate the sandal and flip it with Image > Mirror to make the second one. Make circle shapes in different hues, with different levels of Bevel and Drop Shadow 3-D effects, to create a string of faux beads and pearls to accent smaller photo bordered in black and white. Give the letters an inner bevel. Finish page with title and journaling.

Beach Baby

Angela M. Cable, Rock Springs, Wyoming

Supplies: Image-editing software (Corel Paint Shop Pro 8); fonts (fonttrader.com's Boingo; Garamond)

Beads and rhinestones

Faux plastic beads and rhinestones strung across the page set off candid close-ups in Lauren's digital layout. Make the mats and background with solid-color fill layers and an overlay created with different custom brushes. Create labels in both white and black with typeface and the Text tool. The letters of this typeface are "cut out," so to fill them with white, add white rectangle layers behind the black labels, merge them and then add a touch of a bevel and drop shadow. Create the flower plastic beads as two separate shapes, each with a different Plastic Layer Style added. Create the other plastic beads the same way, but use different shapes and Plastic Layer Styles. Apply a Chrome Layer Style to the hexagon and diamond shapes for rhinestones. Design the brown string with the Line tool and Layer Style. Add deeper drop shadows to the beads to give them depth and dimension.

Just Hannah

Lauren Bavin, Birkenhead, Auckland, New Zealand

Supplies: Image-editing software (Adobe Photoshop CS); fonts (dafont.com's Dymo; misprintedtype.com's Dirty Ego)

Jewels and rhinestones

Wendy creates a textured and torn digital page accented with jewels and rhinestones for her daughter. Create textured background from a pink fill layer by adding large floral and harlequin patterns from dingbat fonts with the Text tool, adjusting the opacity as desired. Merge these layers and apply a denim texture. For the bottle cap, create two circles, the same size and color, each on its own layer. To the top layer circle, apply an Eye Candy Bevel Emboss filter, adjusting the effect to resemble a bottle-cap top. To the lower layer circle, use a round Eraser brush and "cut out" sections along the edge so that it resembles the fluted edge of a bottle cap. Size and position the lower fluted edge to peek out from the beveled top, add text, merge the three layers and add a drop shadow. For the photo anchors, make two small circles, each on a separate layer and "squish" one by changing its perspective to produce one oval and one circle. Position these two layers as desired and merge into one layer; use the Blade Pro plug-in filter to create the beveled metal effect. Create the torn edges with a Distress filter, adjusting the settings for the desired effect. Add title art with the Text tool to complete the layout.

My Baby You'll Be
Wendy Gibson, Mission, British Columbia, Canada

Supplies: Image-editing software (Corel PhotoPaint 8); fonts (1001fonts.com's Flower Ornaments; agfamonotype.com's Monotype Sort; scrapvillage.com's Scriptina, Stamp Act, Typewriter); filters (Flaming Pear Blade Pro; Alien Skin Eye Candy, Xenofex)

Acrylic letters

Ronnie designs a soft digital page with striking faux acrylic letters. Create a white canvas background using the Texturizer filter; drag three photos into position. Use the Eraser tool to remove unwanted portions of the photos then select the Pin Light blend mode to add transparency and light. Add layered word art with varying fonts, sizes, colors and opacities as described in the "Having Fun With Fonts" chapter. Make the acryliclike, glossy letter buttons by drawing a red circle with the Custom Shape tool; duplicate it three times and position the circles with the Move tool. On top of each circle, add a letter to spell "Play." To cut the letter out of the circle, select the letter in the layer palette with <Ctrl> Mouse Click, select the circle beneath the selected letter, choose Edit > Cut, then delete the original letter layer. Repeat this for the other three circles. Apply a downloaded Faux Finish Layer Style to add the glossy disc effect. Use the same Layer Style on the thin frame bordering the page.

Nothing as Lovely as a Child at Play
Ronnie McCray, St. James, Missouri

Supplies: Image-editing software (Adobe Photoshop Elements 2.0); fonts (Hannibal Lector, myfonts.com's P22 Cezanne; Times New Roman); faux finish layer style (adobe.com)

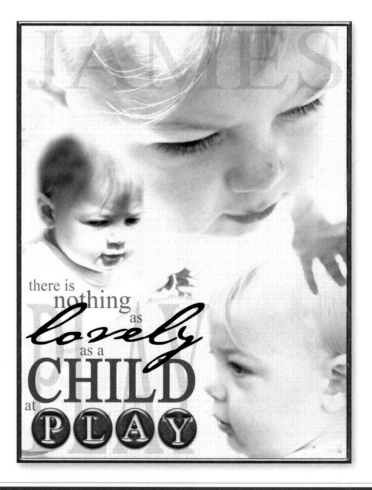

Acrylic-edge watch covers

Ronnie's digital page celebrating her son's love of swimming sports includes some "waterproof" lettering beneath "glass." Create an 8½ x 11" caramel fill layer and add texture by "painting" with different brushes you make or download from the Internet. Use the Eraser tool to add a grunge edge to the focal photo. Blend smaller accent into the background with the Vivid Light blend mode, using the Eraser tool to remove all but child's face. Type in the word "Swim" over the focal photo and duplicate the layer three times; rotate each layer so they are at 90-degree angles from each other and place them in a frame shape and merge into one layer. Make the tag a rectangle, oval and circle—all using a blue sampled from the focal photo with the Color Picker tool; merge these three layers into one. Create brad with a circle shape; apply downloaded Faux Finish Layer Style. Make a rectangle ribbon and add texture. Add text to the tag and ribbon and fade by decreasing the opacity. For watch covers, copy/paste a circle from the water photo. Add black text and a circle with a WOW Clear Plastic Layer Style applied to circles then add a cutout circle custom shape with a Faux Finish Layer Style. Apply slight drop shadows for dimension.

Swim Young Man
Ronnie McCray, St. James, Missouri

Supplies: Image-editing software (Adobe Photoshop Elements 2.0); fonts (dafont.com's Due Date; fonttrader.com's CAC Leslie; Hannibal Lector; myfonts.com's P22 Cezanne; Times New Roman); custom brushes, layer styles (1greeneye.net; adobe.com)

Faux glass watch face

Crackled paper, a lifelike watch element and oversized photos draw you into Ronnie's two-page spread; it's designed as one image but flattened and cut into two separate pages when printed. Create a 24 x 12" taupe background then duplicate it. On the top duplicated layer, add Filter > Render > Clouds and then Filter > Pixelate > Crystallize. Adjust the settings until preferred crackle size is achieved. To accentuate the crackles, select Filter > Stylize > Find Edges. Set blend mode of the layer to Multiply to create a richer crackle texture. Add, size, crop and position photos. Make a rectangle burgundy ribbon shape with a repeated crop of child's face added side by side; cinch the ribbon with Filter > Distort > Pinch. To make the watch, start with a circle and add a Wow Clear Plastic Layer Style to make it look like glass. Add a cutout circle shape on top of that and add a Wow Chrome Layer Style for the rim of the clock. A brush (in a dark brown foreground color) created from a photo of a clock was "stamped" on a tan circle shape. To create the curled photo, drag it onto the layout, size appropriately and add a white border stroke with Edit > Stroke > Width. To add curl, choose Filter > Distort > Shear; pull on the center of the line towards the right until it has the desired curl. Rotate the photo and place it on a layer between the back of the clock and faux glass. Add drop shadows to all photos and elements. Finish with titles and journaling with the Text tool in black, cream and white.

Silent Glory
Ronnie McCray, St. James, Missouri

Supplies: Image-editing software (Adobe Photoshop Elements 2.0); fonts (Hannibal Lector; myfonts.com's P22 Cezanne; Times New Roman); photo distortion tutorial (escrappers.com)

Staples, anchors, eyelets and brads

Melissa creates a tub-play page filled with digital metallic elements. First, make stripes of differing hues with the Custom Shape tool and apply a pattern overlay layer giving a cardstock texture. Design the mats and journaling strips with rectangles, applying a Crumple texture with a filter plug-in. With a white chalk brush, add a cloudy edge to the journaling strips. Use the Typemasking tool to copy and paste "rub a dub" out of the background then add a Drop Shadow Layer Style. Make the label tape in the same way described in "Just Hannah" on page 87. Create the staples and photo anchors with different Custom shapes then add Bevel > Emboss > Drop Shadow Layer Styles. For the metal-rimmed tag, create a textured circle and add a beveled ring of gray around it. Merge the two circles and add a drop shadow and brad. To make brad use a circle with Drop Shadow > Bevel > Emboss > Satin and apply Gradient Overlay. Apply an inner shadow to the text on the tiny tags to make them look punched into the tags. Make the stitching with a brush set to a small size and then draw it with the Paths tool, adding a drop shadow to complete the effect. "Hold" journaling strips in place with a bit of crisscrossed embroidery floss made with two lines and four black "puncture" circles; to the stitches select Bevel > Emboss > Drop Shadows. Add black journaling using the Text tool.

Rub-A-Dub
Melissa Squires, Tecumseh, Michigan

Supplies: Image-editing software (Adobe Photoshop CS); fonts (fontlover.com's Marmalade; fonts.com's Dynamo; myfonts.com's Dolores, Trixie; Urbana, Wolff); crumple filter (Alien Skin Xenofex 2)

Typewriter keys, metal-rimmed tag

Subtle backgrounds and chrome elements set off Ronnie's pool photo in style. Use a Dingbat font's retro flower shape to create a textured background. Add the flower shape and cut out most of the inner portion, leaving a thin flower outline. Duplicate, resize and reposition this flower all over a textured sage fill layer for background. Make the striped rectangular block with varying width rectangles in different coordinating soft shades and then merge into one layer; set layered blocks apart with drop shadows. Design the typewriter keys as described in "Swim Young Man" on page 89, substituting a different font and background color. Create the large, metal-rimmed tag in the same manner, skipping the faux glass cover. Overlap text title layers and the date to finish the page.

Kick-Water Boy
Ronnie McCray, St. James, Missouri
Design inspiration: Gina Cabrera, Phoenix, Arizona

Supplies: Image-editing software (Adobe Photoshop Elements 2.0); fonts (bvfonts.com's 60s Chic; myfonts.com's Pica10 BT, P22 Cezanne; scrapvillage.com's Hootie!)

Paper clip, eyelets, hatpin, metal-rimmed tag

Danielle's digital-accent patriotic page marks a baby's first trip to New York on Independence Day. Use several layered digital papers and elements, making the different torn backgrounds and mats with Brushes, Custom shapes and Texture filters. Tear edges with an Eraser brush and add a white fuzzy layer beneath the torn paper with the Brush tool; merge layers into one. For full control to create bent and curved papers, hand-create custom drop shadows with a light gray Airbrush set at a low opacity. Design the film-strip first as a solid black rectangle, select a smaller rectangle the size of the inside image and hit Delete. Move the same selection down to where the next image should be, hit Delete and repeat. Follow the same procedure for the smaller holes on the sides. Add small numbers along the sides with the Type tool using a bright red hue. Drag photos onto page, with the small ones de-saturated to black-and-white. To hand-tint photo, follow similar steps in "Christmas Gift" on page 68, de-saturating the remaining color a bit more. Create paper clip and grommets with gray fill layers drawn with the Selection tool; cut out inner portions leaving desired finished shapes. Apply Bevel and Emboss Layer Styles for metal look. Select Filter > Render > Lighting Effects for more highlights. Make the metal-rimmed tag as in "Rub-A-Dub" on page 90 using Eraser tool with a round brush tip to make a hole. Design the string with four different gray lines drawn on different layers, paint the drop shadow on and add embossing while erasing portions where it is strung through the hole. Create hatpin with a gray line that is embossed and highlighted like the grommets; add red embossed circle shape and merge with the pin layer. Add title and journaling with grungy typefaces and roughen up even more with different Eraser brushes set at different opacities. Use a ringed circle shape as well the Type and Arc tools to make the faux postage mark on the photo; merge layers into one and apply Stamp filter repeatedly to give it a rubber-stamped look.

Fourth of July
Danielle Catalano-Titus, Woburn, Massachusetts

Supplies: Image-editing software (Adobe Photoshop 7); fonts (oldtype.8m.com's Antique Type; scrapvillage.com's Dirty Bakers Dozen; Impact, Pegsanna HMK)

Anchors, letter charms, nailheads

Vintage plaid draws you into Wendy's page, embellished with a wide array of digital metal accents. Create the plaid with perpendicular thin rectangles set on a tan fill layer; merge all into one layer and apply a Denim texture filter. Tear edges and design photo anchors as described for "My Baby You'll Be" on page 88. To design the crumpled stencil initial, use a taupe rectangle shape and apply Crumple texture with a filter; cut initial out of a crumpled rectangle using a stencil typeface. Apply drop shadows at various depths to add dimension. Make the metal letters and brads with the help of a metal plug-in filter, Text tool and circle shapes.

Farm Girl
Wendy Gibson, Mission, British Columbia

Supplies: Image-editing software (Corel PhotoPaint 8); fonts (fonts.goldenweb.it's Sylfaen; fonttrader.com's 1942 Report; myfonts.com's TimelessT); filters (Auto FX Photo/Graphic Edges 4.0 [grunge edge on photo] and Texturizer [denim]; Flaming Pear Blade Pro's metal; Alien Skin Eye Candy's metal; Alien Skin Xenofex's crumple)

Eyelets, metal-rimmed tag, buckle

Faux metal accents are the perfect addition to Kristie's digital grunge page. Create each of the paper layers, ribbon and paint chip with the same techniques: Draw rectangular shapes in various colors and sizes and age them with custom, hand-drawn brushes in differing shades of gray and cream. Merge layers and apply drop shadows to each separate paper, strip or ribbon. Distress photo with brushwork and Dodge and Burn tools. Apply Chrome Effect filter to the ribbon buckle, grommets and metal-rimmed vellum tags—create as described on "Rub-A-Dub" on page 90; make the vellum effect of the tag by decreasing the opacity of that layer to about 50 percent. Use grungy fonts to complete the distressed feel in the journaling and title border.

Nine Months
Kristie L., Houston, Texas

Supplies: Image-editing software (Adobe Photoshop 7); fonts (dafont.com's Keyboard Plaque, Chelt Press, Misproject, Porcelain; fonts.com's Rage Italic; girlswhowearglasses.com's Oceans11; Garamond); filter (Alien Skin Eye Candy 4000 chrome)

Barbed wire

Barbed wire, mesh and distressed papers fool the eye into believing Jacqueline's page is very old. Start with a sand-colored fill layer and add faint Text in a pencil shade. Use brushes and Dodge and Burn tools to age papers. Create rectangle buttercream and brown paper strips and photo mats, then select Pattern Overlay in the Blending option for each of the layers and choose a pattern from Artist Surfaces to mimic textured cardstock. Age photos by converting to black-and-white; add low opacity brown and yellow fill layers on top of each and manipulate layers with Eraser brushes set at varying opacities and different Blend modes. Design tag and distress it by selecting Filter > Distort > Wave. Make the distressed metal cameo discs as other metal rimmed tags, such as on "Rub-A-Dub" on page 90, using various brushes in darker shades to age edges. To make barbed wire as a separate file, using a hard brush, draw a long straight gray horizontal line with Filter > Noise > Add Noise in Color; then choose Filter > Blur > Motion Blur and drag onto page when finished. Select Filter > Distort > Wave, set Generations 3, Wavelength and Amplitude until desired curve is achieved. Duplicate the layer and rotate for mirror image: Edit > Transform > Flip. With the same brush, draw a lopsided X wherever the lines cross. Finish the wire by applying Bevel and Emboss to each layer, adjusting the settings until a metal sheen is produced; merge layers into one, drag on the page and duplicate. Design brown mesh by stamping a custom brush in brown side by side and merging into one layer; add drop shadows to all layers. Complete with a faint title by applying the Burlap Artist Surfaces pattern to black text.

Cowboy Dreams
Jacqueline Carney, Greenville, Michigan

Supplies: Image-editing software (Adobe Photoshop 7); fonts (scrapvillage.com's PegsannaHMK; Times New Roman)

Hinges

Tonya uses a number of embellishments and layers to give her textured pages depth. Create a cowhide background by using a series of filters (some of them taking more than one application): Render Clouds, Smudge Stick, Jiggle and Fur. Make textured papers with various filters for mats in colors that help the photos pop. To design digital hinges, draw the individual shapes and apply metallic filters before merging into one item. Use rectangle shapes to make the paper tab. Ink edges, add scratches, rickrack and a silver concho to complete the rustic layout.

I Wanna Be a Cowgirl
Tonya Doughty, Wenatchee, Washington

Supplies: Image-editing software (Adobe Photoshop CS); fonts (dafont.com's Kingthings Printingkit; gauchogirl.com's Print); brushes (artist's own)

Bookplate, paper clip

Metal accents adorn Ronnie's digital page dedicated to her son's first day of Kindergarten. Begin with an 8½ x 11" blue background. Create a crosshatch pattern with horizontal and vertical brush strokes in black with white chalking added to the edges. Stamp door image onto the page using a brush made out of a photo. Use two black thin rectangle shapes for upper and lower borders. Drag photo onto blue canvas and add a low, Drop Shadow Layer Style for depth. Create library card with a gray rectangle shape, adding darker gray lines with the Brush tool. To add straight lines, hold down the Shift key when you drag the mouse. Age the edges with different brushes in a darker gray; merge layers and add a slight bevel and drop shadow. Make the paper clip with a custom shape and apply Wow Chrome Shiny Layer. Design the bookplate with a rectangle and two ovals, all merged into one. Cut holes with a round Eraser brush; add sheen and shadow with a Wow Plastic Layer Style. Finish with journaling, title, quote and date using the Text tool.

The Door
Ronnie McCray, St. James, Missouri

Supplies: Image-editing software (Adobe Photoshop Elements 2.0); fonts (myfonts.com's Inspiration; Times New Roman); custom brushes (ti-fi.com)

Silver charms, spiral decorative clip

Kelly uses a great mother/daughter photo as inspiration for this gentle pastel page dressed in charms. Start with a pale blue background. Create brushes in image-editing software to design polka-dot and daisy patterned papers. Use the Rectangular Shape tool to make stripes and duplicate to expedite the process. Enhance the illusion of depth with torn edges created with the Freehand Selection tool and aged with the Burn tool. Create transparent ribbon like paper, but in a narrow rectangular shape with a lower opacity. Add crumpled textures, drop shadows and stitching to various papers; cut tags from blue crumpled paper. Add a torn vellum layer on top of the tags and close with stitching on the envelope. Make a trio of charms using the Custom Shape tool. Set the Shape tool options to Fill Pixels and the foreground color to white. Make each shape on its own layer so they can be modified without affecting one another. Apply a custom Chrome Layer Style downloaded from the Internet. To create spiral decorative clip, create chrome circles in the same manner as charms, duplicate and layer for desired length; position charms to appear hanging from spiral clip. Use the Text tool to add title and journaling to both tags.

My Girl
Kelly Shults, Tulsa, Oklahoma

Supplies: Image-editing software (Adobe Photoshop 7); fonts (typadelic.com's Tweedledee); custom layer style set (Chrome II by Lorne Kwechansky at share.studio.adobe.com)

Bottle caps, nailheads, chrome lettering

Retro fonts, vintage colors and chrome give Angela's layout just the right touch of 1950s nostalgia. Begin with a steel blue background and add red, tan and cream starbursts with the Preset Shape tool's Star1 shape set with a small black outline. Give the vintage photo a hand-tinted look by painting with soft brushes on a new layer, reducing in opacity to lessen the effect. Use the Balls and Bubbles Artistic Effect to create the faux screws, which are enhanced by adding an X with a Cutout 3D Effect applied. To create the bottle caps, select the Gear5 Preset Shape tool. Hold down the shift key while drawing the shape to make a perfectly round image, then apply a Chrome filter > Bevel > Drop Shadow. Design the decals on each bottle cap with hand-drawn shapes and fontwork. Add virtual vellum and fabric tape with the rectangular shape tool. Complete layout with black and white journaling using the Text tool.

Of Men and Cars
Angela M. Cable, Rock Springs, Wyoming

Supplies: Image-editing software (Corel Paint Shop Pro 8); fonts (Arial; dafont.com's Hood Ornament; fonttrader.com's Copperplate); plug-in filters (Alien Skin Eye Candy 4000; Flaming Pear Super Blade Pro); automobile logo (source unknown)

Wooden letters, photo corners, brads

Ronnie's limited color palette creates a coordinated layout to showcase a cute photo and polished wooden accents. Design distressed patterned papers with brushes for background. Enhance photo using the Cloning tool to remove any distracting areas of swimming pool behind subject's head. For wooden initial, photo corners and brad, apply Layer Style to create the look of polished wood. Reiterate water theme by making a paper-pieced-look sailboat tag, then stamp the sailboat subtly on the journaling tag and add journaling in white text. Add title using Text tool, rotate and drag into position.

Clap and Play
Ronnie McCray, St. James, Missouri

Supplies: Image-editing software (Adobe Photoshop Elements 2.0); fonts (Hannibal Lector, Times New Roman); brushes (1greeneye.net; paintillusion.com)

Wooden slide mount, buckle

Old-fashioned wooden page accents lend a nostalgic look to Ronnie's page featuring her son's contemporary passion. Begin with a color-blocked background and striped patterned paper created with the Line tool. Use the Rectangle shape to design wooden accents; apply a Polished Wood Layer Style and adds ribbons attached to a buckle as a dividing element. Create a toy car and a vintage car brush from actual photos. Turn the toy car brush semitransparent and place over the slide mount to simulate a transparency adhered over a slide mount. Finish with titles and journaling in various fonts.

Fascination
Ronnie McCray, St. James, Missouri

Supplies: Image-editing software (Adobe Photoshop Elements 2.0); fonts (Hannibal Lector, Hootie!, Times New Roman)

Barn wood

Tonya's rustic wood accents provide the perfect backdrop for sage advice to her daughter. Start with a "file folder" over the background using Rectangle shapes. Add textured paper created by a brush with color pulled from photo; use brush to smudge edges onto manila folder for grunge look. Add saturated and de-saturated photos. Highlight the most important words of title featuring them on wood tags or as wooden letters. Design the wooden elements using the Shape tool; apply a Wood filter and modify its default settings to get a weathered barn-wood look. Tonya used a Layer Style she created herself to make the letters look burned into the wooden tags. Accent art with faux digital staples and a ribbon. Wrap title across the top and down the side and add journaling to complete the page.

Be The You You Are
Tonya Doughty, Wenatchee, Washington

Supplies: Image-editing software (Adobe Photoshop CS), fonts (letterindelights.com's LD Remington; Stomper); brushes (artist's own designs); filters (Alien Skin Eye Candy 4000)

Wooden clothespins

Ronnie creates the perfect digital elements to accent fun photos of her sons in the laundry basket. Begin with a textured and distressed color-block background. See "Silent Glory" on page 89 for instructions on how to curl a photo; drag photos to background. Design clothing label with rectangular shapes and Text tool. Use Shape tool to create two different clothespins; remove unwanted areas with an Eraser to define detail and add metal lines and circle shapes for clothespin springs. Clone or duplicate clothespins for number desired. Add "washing instructions" and journaling to finish thematic layout.

Stinky, Dirty Boys
Ronnie McCray, St. James, Missouri

Supplies: Image-editing software (Adobe Photoshop Elements 2.0), font (Hank BT)

Leather

Kim's leather bookplate is a great addition to an outdoorsy page rich in depth and texture. Begin with a background of solid, aged, crimped and patterned papers; create texture by adding filter effects—such as Canvas and Cardboard—to various colored rectangle shapes, then smudge with brushes and add stitches using Line tool. Place photo. Make the grungy leather bookplate with a custom shape and apply Leather texture. Use Corel Draw and PhotoPaint to enlist the help of a plug-in filter to create plaid patterned ribbons, pinching them to a smaller width where strung through a hole of bookplate. Create metal brads using a gradient, circular Shape and Plastic filter. Add drop shadows and bevels to every element in varying degrees for depth and dimension.

Ally Aka Bubs
Kim Liddiard, Northglenn, Colorado

Supplies: Image-editing software (Corel Draw 12, PhotoPaint 12); fonts (cosmi.com's 1000 Best Fonts CD: Adler, Anhedonia, Big Fish Ensemble, Cuomotype, FrouFrou, Romeo); plaid filter (unknown source)

Leather and rope

Tonya designs leather and rope accents to complement the outdoorsy, western theme of her photos. Start with a textured, floral embossed background. Create the leather mats and photo corners by first drawing their shape and then applying a Leather filter with default properties altered to achieve the look you desire. Layer the leather and photos above background, then anchor them by lacing lengths of rope through large copper grommets. To create rope, use filters to generate the stripe pattern then rotate the lines diagonally; crop out a narrow section and distort it so it isn't perfectly straight. Apply Emboss and Shadow effects to create a 3-D look and round the ends using the Eraser to make them appear to go into the grommets.

Just Like Me
Tonya Doughty, Wenatchee, Washington

Supplies: Image-editing software (Adobe Photoshop CS), fonts (letteringdelights.com's LD Remington, LD Letterpress); brushes (artist's own designs); filters (Alien Skin Eye Candy 4000)

Pressed flowers

Michelle creates a bright, beautiful and feminine page to showcase photos of her daughter's passion for the family's favorite garden site and the beginning of her own interest in photography. First, apply texture to paper and remove the white background from the photos, adjusting the blend mode to Multiply and lowering the opacity to 50 percent to allow the paper's texture to show. Apply a grungy edge to photos to complement the organic feel of the page. For pressed-flower accent, start with a flower photo. Remove flower from its background, add a drop shadow and paint with a stipple brush around the edges. Create a daisy brush and stamp it on faux vellum for an additional embellishment. Add the photos, stitching, journaling and title to complete page.

A Quest for All Things Beautiful
Michelle Shefveland, Sauk Rapids, Minnesota

Supplies: Image-editing software (Adobe Photoshop Elements 2.0, Jasc Paintshop Pro 8.1, Microsoft Digital Image Pro 9); fonts (Allembert, Codex Text, Misproject, Porcelain); filters (Auto FX Photo's Graphic Edges)

Shells, ferns

Just because you are a digital scrapbooker doesn't mean you can use ONLY digital elements in your pages. Sheila drew the Sea Oats, or the fan-shaped grass, and then scanned them in as line art. Begin with your own hand-drawn sea grass or copyright-free clip art. Create custom brushes of the art and stamp them as elements on the background paper. Scan in small, flat shells and turn them into custom brushes as well. Use the shells as accents on top of the paper, in the vellum envelope and as part of the texture of the background. Import the photo and put inside an oval frame; decorate with stamped shells. Complete the layout with title, journaling quote and date stamp.

Freda & Olive
Sheila McIntosh Dixon, Milton, Florida

Supplies: Image-editing software (Jasc Paintshop Pro 8, Microsoft Digital Image Pro 9); font (Stamp Act); brushes (Jasc Paintshop Pro 8 and artist's own designs)

Printed ribbon

Faux printed ribbon accents look great as a border on Ronnie's digital page. If you look closely at the photo, you'll notice the reflection of Ronnie's son James as he looks through the sliding glass door to the family dog, Chrissy. Because the reflection is subtle, Ronnie uses the brick red color from the reflection as the background color behind this portion of the photo. This helps the viewer to find it as the eye will jump to the patch of similar color. Build a background of color textures and patterns, then layer duplicate photos on it. Add page accents, clip art paw prints and title and journaling to complete the page.

Dog & Boy Bond
Ronnie McCray, St. James, Missouri

Supplies: Image-editing software (Adobe Photoshop Elements 2.0); fonts (2P's Roxie, Weathervane; Esat Hoxha, Hank BT, Times New Roman)

Clothing label

The clothing-label inspiration for this page was the photo of Chelsea's sons as they met for the first time. Start with a black-and-white to put the focus on the precious moment captured and then created a textured, vibrant, solid-colored background to balance it. Next, create a custom clothes tag with the Shape tool and add journaling. Repeat the title using a Transparent Fade effect for subtle, shadowed emphasis.

Brothers Forever
Chelsea Clement, Thibodaux, Louisiana

Supplies: Image-editing software (Microsoft Digital Image Pro 10); fonts (Arial, Blackadder ITC, Brickley Script)

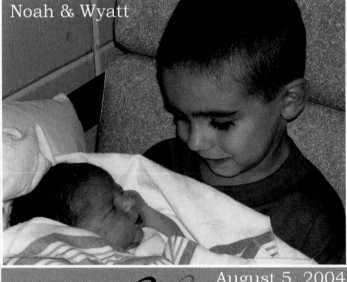

Twisted ribbon

This page has all the right parts for a fun, summer layout: great bright pics, summery colors, cute accents. What it also has is a dynamic curled ribbon lending movement to the page. Ronnie uses the ribbon to "tie" the layout together and the metal ring in the center draws the eye right to Isaac, the subject of the page. The curls in the ribbon give the impression of the water waves and adds that little "something special" to make this digital page anything but flat! The technique: Hand-draw the rolled edges and use a paintbrush to paint in the shadows. Use the Distort > Liquefy filter to make the ribbon smaller as it leads into and out of the rolled section.

Splash Zone
Ronnie McCray, St. James, Missouri

Supplies: Image-editing software (Adobe Photoshop Elements 2.0); fonts (Hannibal Lector, Cheltpress Trial, Times New Roman); curled ribbon technique (courtesy of Lauren Bavin)

Gingham ribbon, adhesive bandage

A friend once asked Melyssa what she felt was the hardest thing about being a parent. Months later, she saw this photo and the answer suddenly came to her, leading to this layout. By keeping the page clean, the focus remains on the photo and the heartfelt journaling. The bandage element, despite being nontraditional, is the perfect accompaniment and is created by using the Marquee tool to draw a rectangle filled with R202, G184, B166. Round the corners using the Lasso tool. To create the dimples, use a darker version of the bandage color and, with a soft edge brush on its own layer, create the indentations. Every other row of dots should line up. When you are satisfied with the arrangement of dots, apply the Bevel/Emboss filter. Select and copy the center rectangle piece, add an additional bevel and merge the layers together. Duplicate completed bandage and, if desired, cut out the "X" and "O" initials from the centers.

Hardest Thing About Being a Parent
Melyssa Connolly, Truro, Nova Scotia, Canada

Supplies: Image-editing software (Adobe Photoshop 7.0), fonts (dafont.com's Felix Titling; Engravers MT, Scriptina)

THE HARDEST THING ABOUT BEING A *Parent*

I really coundn't think of one particular thing, until you the day we took you to the hospital for your surgery. I felt so hopeless sitting there and not being able to make the pain go away. That is the hardest thing in the world about being a parent, watching your child hurt and not being able to stop the pain.

Fabric, ribbon, lace

In true shabby chic style, Lauren layered several pink, distressed and torn papers to create this warm and feminine background. Create a floral brush and use to stamp the lace, then add a drop shadow and embossing to give it the 3-D appearance. Design buttons, using a Layer Style, and ribbons, all mainstays of the shabby chic style. Metallic accents and a dangling stencil number complete the page. For the title, begin with the simple font, then rasterize it and erase portions with a grungy brush to give it a distressed look.

Moody
Lauren Bavin, Birkenhead, Auckland, New Zealand

Supplies: Image-editing software (Adobe Photoshop 7.0, digitalscrabookplace.com); fonts (larabiefonts.com's Gunplay)

Fibers

Roseanne wanted to create a delicate page to showcase her beautiful, hand-tinted photo (which she made by using the colorize brush to paint in sections of her grayscale photo). Create a first layer that is softly textured over pale-pink background with a gridlike pattern of warm, fuzzy fibers for detail. Create the fibers by using Brushes and then duplicating the fiber over and over to create the grid. Design vellum for the journaling block by lowering the opacity of a white rectangle and "pin" in place. "Wrap" additional fibers around the mat and gather in the center by passing through a silver heart charm. For the charm, make a Custom Shape. Apply a Pewter Layer Style and a Drop Shadow before adding "pearls" made from circles with a Pearl Layer Style added. The resulting page is a tender, heritage-style complement to the old-fashioned-looking photo.

Cherub
Roseanne Miske, Monument, Colorado

Supplies: Image-editing software (Adobe Photoshop CS); font (source unknown)

Cherub
1. a type of angel characterized as a chubby, rosy cheeked child with wings
2. a child with a sweet, innocent face

Sela at 8 months

Fibers

Doris lavishly layers many different ribbons over the pastel background to create this flirty, fun, feminine page. Vellum slide mounts showcase accent photos to help tell the story of Michaela's first birthday. A sheer pink layer above the background adds additional warmth, and pearly pink buttons help anchor the main photo in this sweet layout. While these elements are available as downloads, use them also as inspiration for experimentation in designing your own.

Michaela's First Birthday
Doris Castle, Fonda, New York

Supplies: Image-editing software (Adobe Photoshop CS); fonts (Giddyup), Digital Papers and Elements (Creative Pixels CD by Kim Liddiard, thecreativepixel.com)

Curled ribbon

One of the advantages of digital scrapbooking is the availability of filters to help create realistic elements such as those Sally uses here. Create the perky, pink plaid using a Tartan Fabric filter and then give it a torn, frayed edge where it acts as a giant corner to the entire page. Attach it with digital faux stitches and delicate pink and gold heart brads. Add a layer of textured-squares on the background and tiny stitches around the border. Use special effects filters to create the extremely realistic curled ribbons dangling from a journaling block. Finish layout with title and journaling.

Mahkayla-baby Sweet
Sally Beacham, East Waterboro, Maine

Supplies: Image-editing software (Jasc Paintshop Pro 9.0); fonts (2P's Wonderful, Little Buddy; Bradley Hand); filters (Auto FX DreamSuite, Alien Skin Xenofex 2, AV Bros Page Curl, Geomantics Fabric Weaver)

Shredded ribbon, rickrack

Doris creates masses of curly ribbons to extend the photo theme of her daughter Alyssa playing with gift ribbon beyond the borders of the photo and out onto the page. Start with a layered and torn background using patterns similar to those in the photo. Draw the curls with brushes and add Shadow and Emboss filters for depth and sheen. Add rickrack as a fun, feminine embellishment. Stamp a flower across the layout and add a quote tags and multilayer to finish the page.

Life Is a Wonderous Gift
Doris Castle, Fonda, New York

Supplies: Image-editing software (Adobe Photoshop CS); fonts (source unknown)

Organza, satin ribbon, tulle

When Lauren saw a paper layout using gathered tulle, she challenged herself to recreate the effect digitally. And having previously created digital tulle, she had a good starting point. She first created a rectangular shape filled with a small diamond pattern and applied beveling and a drop shadow for depth. Duplicate the layer and use the Distort > Liquefy filter to gather each layer separately. At the point that the tulle is gathered, add a small button or ribbon bow for accent.

Hannah Rose
Lauren Bavin, Birkenhead, Auckland, New Zealand

Supplies: Image-editing software (Adobe Photoshop 7.0)

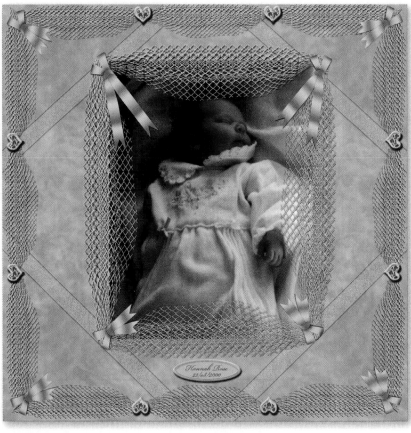

Applique rosettes, lace binding tape, sheer ribbon

Doris uses several textile embellishments to create a delicate digital layout. Use the image-editing software's Shape tools, Eraser tool and create custom Brushes to design background and elements in layers. Gather ribbons, made sheer by varying opacity, in a floral bow and add a wide lace "binding tape" border for soft accents. Make a date plate and delicate appliqué rosette to dangle from tiny pink ribbons. Use Bevel and Emboss filters and Drop Shadows to add depth and dimension to all page elements. Complete the layout with title and journaling.

Sweet Baby Michaela
Doris Castle, Fonda, New York

Supplies: Image-editing software (Adobe Photoshop CS), fonts (Aldine 402, Freehand 529); brushes (artist's own)

Sweet
Baby MICHAELA

Michaela may be your given name, but you are lovingly referred to in many ways such as Kaylee, Kaylee Bird, Kaylee Fish, Baby Boo and of course as Sweet Baby Michaela.

You were named after your grandfather Michael, and it is wonderful to see his resemblance every time I look at you.

YOUR NAME IS A CONNECTION TO YOUR HERITAGE.

2003

farm FRESH
Thank God, I'm a Country Boy

It takes a set of parents that were raised in the country to allow their baby to run around the front yard with just his diaper.

THANKGOD

James

July 29, 2004

Rope, bandanna

It's hard to believe that Ronnie's farm-fresh elements are entirely digital! Design the chicken wire with a series of shapes arranged in the proper order and then make 3-D with a Layer Style. Add the tractor and rooster with brushes and crop the handkerchief from a digital or scanned photo. Even the rope, which Ronnie originally created using a feature in Microsoft Picture It, was opened in Photoshop Elements and aged using the Burn tool and Noise filter. Add a layered title and journaling to finish the page.

Farm Fresh
Ronnie McCray, St. James, Missouri

Supplies: Image-editing software (Adobe Photoshop Elements 2.0, Microsoft Picture It! Photo Version 6.0); fonts (CAC Leslie, Hannibal Lector, Hootie!, Times New Roman)

Organizing and storing digital photos & layouts

Digital photography and computer scrapbooking are really mixed blessings. You can take literally hundreds of photographs and create hundreds of computer scrapbook pages at little to no cost whatsoever. The ripple effect of this creative scenario for a die-hard scrapbook enthusiast can be frustration at the sorting, organizing, choosing and storing of the photos and art. If you're not careful, you could easily end up with thousands of photos and computer scrapbook pages spread haphazardly all over your hard drive, taking up memory and making it hard to find other things you might really need. Key to your enjoyment of computer scrapbooking is a good system for storage and organization.

Choose a software storage program

There are numerous photo-storage programs available to store and organize your digital images. In fact, most cameras come with some type of software for both storage and editing.

Decide what to keep

It is tempting to keep all your photos, especially when the cost of storing digital images is so minimal. However, storing bad digital photos will only create frustration when you sit down to scrapbook. Make deleting the bad photos a priority when you download from your camera to your image-storage software.

This is also a good time to determine which photos can be fixed. Before you delete a "bad" photo, remember that image-editing software can fix color, brightness and more and allows you to crop a poorly composed photo. If you decide the photograph is worth saving, make any necessary enhancements before you store it.

Create a naming system

One of the most important decisions you will make in the digital-image-organization process is deciding how to label your photos.

Choose a simple and consistent naming system that you will remember and will allow you to retrieve your photos quickly. Because chronological order is the most natural path the human brain travels when retrieving information, begin your photo labels with the year. Next, specify an event and add a topic. This system will group photos together by year and event, then clarify by subject. For example, name all of last year's Christmas photos as 2004_xmas_topic.tif. Likewise, store any computer scrapbook pages made with those photos together in the same folder prior to to burning the images to CD.

CDs and DVDs

Burning images and art onto CDs is probably the most common method for storing digital photos. It is easy, inexpensive and compact. Quality CDs from reputable product manufacturers will remain light- and heat-stable for a century or more. CDs use a marking system, which is both larger and spread farther apart than a DVD, which allows them to be more tolerant of scratches. Store your disks much like regular photos—away from excessive light, heat and humidity. They should be kept in plastic cases that will prevent scratching.

Keep organized with Fellowes' Compact Disc Multi-Media Drawer, CD/DVD Labeling Starter Kit and Maxell Slims CD Cases.

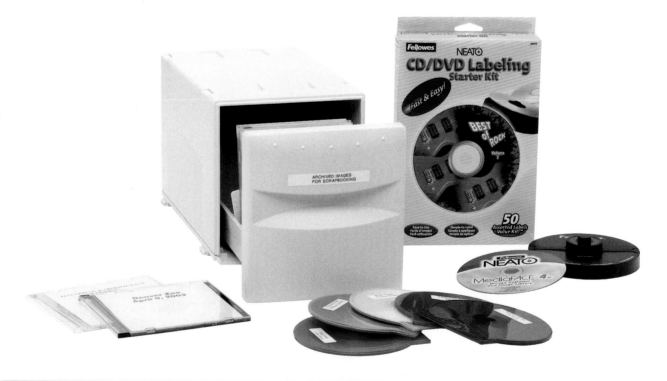

Online storage

Many online photo-processing companies offer photo storage. This will free up space on your hard drive and reduce the number of CDs you have to store. The concerns with this method are what happens if that photo processor goes out of business and who can gain access to my photos? Most companies offer password-protected access and assurances that you are the only one with the ability to view your photos.

Extra hard drive

An extra hard drive is not completely uncommon with die-hard digital photographers and scrapbookers. It can be very efficient in terms of the virtually limitless number of photographs you can store on it.

Take the time to organize and store your digital photos and computer-generated scrapbook pages using a system that is simple and consistent. This will ensure accessibility to your photos and art so you can easily access, enjoy and share them with others.

Sharing your digital artwork

One of the biggest rewards of computer scrapbooking is the joy of sharing the digital art with others. Some scrapbookers print their pages onto archival photo paper, slip them into page protectors and then into scrapbook albums.

If your desire is to share your computer-generated pages in the digitial realm of the Internet, there are a number of ways to do so after you've saved your layouts. When saving your layouts, many scrapbookers prefer to save two versions of the finished pages: a high-resolution version and a low-resolution version.

High-resolution layouts, created and saved at 300dpi, will be ready for printing onto photo paper any time you need them. Save a low-resolution version of the original art at 72dpi for viewing on private Web sites, public digital-scrapbooking forums, sending as e-mail attachments and more.

A good number of digital camera and image-editing software packages also include powerful tools for organizing and sharing artwork, creating cards and calendars, sharing images on mobile phones and PDAs, burning CD slide shows for TV viewing and automatic backing-up of photos onto CD.

However you choose to share your computer-generated masterpieces, one thing is certain: They will wow and amaze anyone who sees them!

ScrappyDoodles.com's Online Digital Scrapbook and Do-It-Yourself Pro Website Creator is another great option for creating scrapbook pages and sharing them on the World Wide Web.

Smart and simple software that makes creating, organizing and sharing computer scrapbook layouts a breeze are Nova Development's Photo Explosion Deluxe and Jasc's Paint Shop Photo Album 5 Deluxe Edition.

Basic image-editing tool icons and tasks

These are tools from Adobe Photoshop Elements CS. You will find many of the same or similar tools in your own image-editing software. Perhaps the icons will be a little different, but the tasks they perform are relatively the same. Getting to know your image-editing software's tools and functions will help make computer scrapbooking quick and easy!

Tools

 Rectangular marquee
Use this tool to make a rectangular selection on your image. Hidden tools: Elliptical marquee: Use to make circular and oval selections.

 Lasso
Use to make a freehand selection around a part of your image. Hidden tools: Polygon Lasso and Magnetic Lasso.

 Selection brush
Use to brush in area to be selected.

 Custom shape
Rectangle tool: Use to draw a rectangle on the page. Hidden tools include: Line tool: Use to draw lines. Shape selection tool: Use to select shapes of choice.

 Paint bucket
Use to flood an enclosed area of your image with color of choice.

 Brush
Use to paint on the image using the foreground color as the paint color.

 Eraser
Use to erase parts of the image. On the background layer, erasing replaces the image with the background color. On a layer, erasing the image removes it completely, allowing other layers below to show through. Hidden tools: Background Eraser: Use to remove the background detail.

 Blur
Use to blur by dragging over area of image you want blurred.

 Sponge
Use to subtly change color saturation or vividness of an image area.

 Dodge
Use to add brightness. Effective in adding dimension and shadows.

 Clone stamp
Use to retouch an image by copying an area of an image and stamping it over another. Hidden tools: Pattern Stamp: Use to paint with a pattern you select.

 Hand
Use to view another area of the image.

 Foreground color
Click this color to open the Color Picker to choose another color for the foreground.

Background color
Click this color to open the Color Picker to choose another color for the background.

Switch colors
Click arrows to switch from foreground to background color and vice versa.

Move
Use to move a layer or the selected area to a new position on the image.

Magic wand
Use to select areas in the image by selecting areas of similar color.

Crop
Use to select an area of the image which you want to retain (the area outside this is discarded).

Type
Click to type text onto your image. Press Enter to start a new line. Hidden tools include: Vertical Type tool for creating vertical type.

Gradient
Use to fill an area with a blend of two or more colors of choice.

Pencil
Use to draw freehand lines on the image.

Red-eye brush
Use to remove red-eye from people and animals in images.

Sharpen
Use this to increase the clarity of edges in an image.

Smudge
Use to smudge colors in an image.

Burn
Use to darken areas of the image, adding shadows and dimension.

Eyedropper
Use this to sample colors from your image to use to paint or fill areas, etc. Click the Eyedropper and then hold it over an area of your image and click to select the color under the mouse cursor as the foreground color.

Zoom
Click to select the tool, then click on the image to zoom in. Hold the Alt key as you click to zoom out.

Glossary

Bevel

In image-editing software, a chamfered edge that can be applied to type, buttons or selections to emphasize a three-dimensional effect.

Bitmap

An array of values specifying the color of every single pixel in a digital image.

Brightness

Refers to how light or dark an image appears to be.

Burning

Recording data onto a CD-ROM using a CD burner or recorder.

Clip art

Collections of typically royalty-free illustrations.

CMYK

Cyan, magenta, yellow and black. Refers to the subtractive color theory and inks used in digital printing.

Contrast

The difference between the dark areas and light areas in an image.

Digitize

To convert anything—such as text, photographs and scanned documents and objects—into a binary form so that it can be digitally processed or manipulated.

Dingbat

The modern name for fonts of decorative symbols and ornaments.

Dots per inch (dpi)

A unit of measurement used to represent the resolution of devices such as printers.

Download

To transfer images or fonts from a remote computer, Internet server or Web site to your own computer desktop.

Export

A feature in many software applications that allows you to save a file in a format so that it can be used by another application or operating system.

File format

The way a program arranges data so that it can be stored or displayed on a computer, such as JPEG or EPS.

Font

Set of characters sharing the same typeface style and size.

Icon

An onscreen illustration of an object, such as a tool, CD or folder.

Kerning

The adjustment of spacing between two type characters.

Palette

Refers to the subset of colors that are needed to display an image properly or the submenus in image-editing software programs that allows you to select colors, swatches and more.

Pixel (picture element)

The smallest component of any digitally generated image.

Resolution

The degree of quality, clarity and definition captured in a digital image or with which an image is reproduced.

RGB

Red, green, blue. Refers to additive color.

Additional instructions & credits

Page 1 Hikin'
Nick Nyffeler, Memory Makers Books

Page 3 Bookplate/ dedication
Nick Nyffeler, Memory Makers Books

Page 4 Amazing Grace
Page Design: Robin Rozum, Memory Makers Books; Photos: MaryJo Regier, Memory Makers Books

Page 11 Pieces Of You
Tonya Doughty, Wenatchee, Washington

Pages 14-17 Making Your First Page
MaryJo Regier, Memory Makers Books

Supplies: Image-editing software (Adobe Photoshop CS)

Page 20 Confucius Say

Tonya created all the elements and papers on this page using her image-editing software. She then layered the supplies and added drop shadows and other details. Designing your own elements and papers takes a little practice, but it can be well worth it. You can create entire themes that work with your quote or idea. Coloring is important as well. If you want the theme to be obvious at first glance, minimize any distracting colors, especially in your foreground photos. Add textures to your elements and place them at different angles for a more dramatic effect.

Tonya Doughty, Wenatchee, Washington

Supplies: Image editing software (Adobe Photoshop CS); fonts (Chinese Rocks, Kingthings Printingkit – Dirty Ego)

Page 44 Blessed

Use image adjustments to colorize photos. To change the overall coloring of the main photo, Veronica used the Hue/Saturation and Levels features. By using these adjustments, you can age a photo or brighten a photo easily. After selecting a colorization for your main photo, be sure to keep the colors in the rest of the page similar. Select three main colors and work with these. To get a more exact match, use the Eyedropper tool to choose the shades you want from the larger photo. Avoid too much monotony by selecting one bright accent color to draw your eye to a word or element on the page but don't add any other color photo. If you add more pictures, de-saturate them and use the Levels adjustment to lighten them so that the page doesn't become too dark. Separate text from images into blocks separated by brushes or shapes. Add the Bevel/Emboss feature to your title to give it depth.

Veronica Ponce, Miami, Florida

Supplies: Image-editing software (Adobe Photoshop CS); fonts (1942 Report, misprintedtype.com's Brush; Misproject)

Page 66 Silly Sebastian

Don't be afraid to add different fonts to your pages. Fonts really add to the feel of the page so it's important to stick with those that best set the mood. In this page, Veronica placed words in different layers and changed the opacities so they weren't competing with each other. Simulate this look by choosing one dramatic font for the word that best describes the theme of your page. Use a different color for the word you want to highlight, and add a Drop Shadow or Bevel/Emboss for even more impact. Never use fonts that overpower each other. There should be one definitive font for emphasis and the others should just complement it.

Veronica Ponce, Miami, Florida

Supplies: Image-editing software (Adobe Photoshop CS); fonts (Century Gothic, Crack Babies, myfonts. com's P22 Cezanne)

Page 84 Rugged Young Man

Khaki hues, rich textured accents, air-brushed title, and a faux "outdoors" photo make up Ronnie McCray's 8½ x 11" page. Using the Selection tool, she first went to work on the photo of her son, removing the background and replacing it with a treetop scene (similar steps followed to give the cutout look to the daisy photo). She then merged these two layers, becoming one. Using Colorize and Duplicate Layer functions, plus the Eraser tool, she changed the hue of his shirt to sepia. The background was created with a fill layer in tan, adding a texture filter. Striped paper was created with a duplicate fill layer to which rust stripes were added with the Rectangular Shape tool. For the Belted O-ring, Ronnie used a wrinkled Leather Layer Style for the leather strip, then used the Dodge and Burn tool to give it a wrinkled look. The stitching on the leather strap was created by using a thin-lined brush. A Wood Layer Style was applied to the O-ring shape. The wood tag was cut from a photo of a piece of plywood in a tag shape. Brads are created with a circle shape and Plastic Layer Style. For the chain on the wood tag, little circles are lined up in a chain shape, with a WOW Chrome Layer Style applied to each one. A slight Drop Shadow Layer Style is applied to all the papers, photos, and elements. For the finishing touch, a frame of four text layers (rotated to make a square) is added to bring focus to his face and the title is given an air-brushed stencil effect. To create the reverse text look, Ronnie used the Type Selection tool to add the text, then Selection > Invert. To this selection she "sprayed" with a soft-edged Paintbrush tool.

Ronnie McCray, St. James, Missouri

Supplies: Image-editing software (Adobe Photoshop Elements 2.0, Microsoft Picture It! 6); fonts (2P's Jack Frost; dafont.com's Due Date; myfonts.com's P22 Cezanne; Times New Roman)

Sources

The following companies manufacture products featured in this book. Please check your local retailers to find these materials, or go to a company's Web site for the latest product. In addition, we have made every attempt to properly credit the items mentioned in this book. We apologize to any company that we have listed incorrectly, and we would appreciate hearing from you.

20/20- no contact info

ACD Systems
(250) 544-6700
www.acdsystems.com

Adobe Systems, Inc.
(866) 766-2256
www.adobe.com

Alien Skin Software, LLC
(888) 921-SKIN
www.alienskin.com

ArcSoft®, Inc.
(510) 440-9901
www.arcsoft.com

Auto FX Software
(205) 980-0056
www.autofx.com

Broderbund Software
(319) 247-3325
www.broderbund.com

Canon U.S.A., Inc.
(516) 328-5000
www.canon.com

Concord Camera Corp.
(954) 331-4200
www.concord-camera.com

Corel Corporation
(800) 772-6735
www.corel.com

CottageArts.net™
(320) 230-3743
www.cottagearts.net

Creating Keepsakes
(888) 247-3325
www.creatingkeepsakes.com

Digital Scrapbook Place LLC, The
(866) 396-6906
www.digitalscrapbookplace.com

Eastman Kodak Company
(770) 522-2542
www.kodak.com

Epson America, Inc.
(562) 981-3840
www.epson.com

Extensis™, Inc.
(800) 796-9798
www.extensis.com

Fellowes, Inc.
(800) 955-0959
www.fellowes.com

Flaming Pear
www.flamingpear.com

Fuji Photo Film U.S.A., Inc.
(800) 755-3854
www.fujifilm.com

Gauchogirl Creative
gauchogirl@gauchogirl.com
www.gauchogirl.com

Hewlett-Packard Company
www.hp.com/go/scrapbooking

Ilford Imaging USA, Inc.
(888) 727-4751
www.printasiafun.com

Janlynn® Corporation of America
(800) 445-5565
www.janlynn.com

Jasc Software
(800) 622-2793
www.jasc.com

Kaleidoscope Collections, LLC
(970) 231-4076
www.kaleidoscopecollections.com

Konica Minolta Photo Imaging U.S.A., Inc.
(800) 285-6422
www.konicaminolta.com

Krylon®
(216) 566-200
www.krylon.com

Lineco, Inc.
(800) 322-7775
www.lineco.com

Maxell Corporation of America
(800) 533-2836
www.maxell.com

Micrografx®
(972) 234-1769
www.micrografx.com

Microsoft Corporation
www.microsoft.com

Nikon™
www.nikon.com

Nova Development Corporation
(818) 591-9600
www.novadevelopment.com

Provo Craft®
(888) 577-3545
www.provocraft.com

Roxio
(905) 482-5200
www.roxio.com

Scrappy Doodles
(918) 280-4540
www.scrappydoodles.com

vintage workshop™, LLC, the
(913) 341-5559
www.thevintageworkshop.com

Ulead
(877) 226-6776
www.ulead.com

Font websites

1001fonts.com

acidfonts.com

acme.com

agfamonotype.com

byfonts.com

cosmic.com

creatingkeepsakes.com

dafont.com

flyerstarter.com

font.com

fontdiner.com

fontfreak.com

fontlovers.com

fontmenu.com

fonts.com

fonts.goldenweb.it

fontseek.com

fonttrader.com

gauchogirl.com

girlswhowearglasses.com

grsites.com

highfonts.com

letteringdelights.com

misprintedtype.com

myfonts.com

oldtype.8m.com

pccrafter.com

pixelnook.home.comcast.net

scrapbookvillage.com

simplythebest.net

twopeasinabucket.com

typadelic.com

unionfonts.com

webfxmall.com

webpagepublicity.com

westwindfonts.com

Index